THE HENRY`S AT SEA

HENRY MACMILLAN WRIGHT

THE HENRY'S

ACKNOWLEDGEMENTS

I want to thank those many people that told me I should write this book.

Thanks to Ginny Wright for her school marm skills in cleaning up my original draft and for her encouragement.

Thanks to Charlotte Buckley, especially for her computer help and putting up with me.

Thanks to my daughter Virginia Strickland for her advice and typing.

Thanks to Henry Jr. for his memory and input and encouragements. The book came alive over and over.

I dedicate The Henry's to my five beautiful granddaughters in hopes they will enjoy remembering their Pappy, and their Dad and Uncle when he was teenager.

TABLE OF CONTENTS

A Father Son Adventure

Waves as high as telephone poles. Tossing our forty-one foot sloop TAIS around like a kid riding a surfboard. These waves were the result of a week of forty five knot winds out of the north (of Madeira) unencumbered by any land for a few thousand miles.

Madeira sits about four hundred miles out in the Atlantic off the coast of Spain. With waves, scary big, we wondered, should we venture out of the protected breakwater? We had been waiting a week for the winds to subside. Time was running short. We had to be in Gran Canarie (Canary Islands) for the start of the first trans-Atlantic race for cruisers. The Canary Islands were a two-day sail to the south. We had to be there. We voted, *Yes, let's go!*

THE IDEA

It all began when I was a child, maybe six. You see, I was programmed to go to sea at some time in my life. One of my early memories of my father was lying on the glider on the back porch. One particular dark night it was very stormy. We were in the glider just my "father" and me. We never called him "Dad." Despite the lightning and thunder and wind, I felt comforted and safe. We made believe we were on a boat at sea with big waves all around. I could see and feel this scene as we were swinging in the glider. This was very real to me, a kid being on the high seas.

I was sick in bed once when I was about twenty. My mother brought me *Family at Sea* to read. This was a book about a couple and two children sailing around the world in a thirty two foot ketch. I loved it! I was right with John Caldwell and his family on the boat. Later in our voyage we met John at Palm Island in the Southern Caribbean. It was a delightful visit with my teenage hero! He owned a concession on the beach. A cruise ship came in and anchored letting 500 people off on this tiny island. John was so busy mixing drinks we could no longer talk to him, so we left the tiny island.

As I grew up I heard stories about my swashbuckling great great grandfather John Newland Maffitt who was a blockade runner out of Wilmington. *Sea Devil of the Confederacy* was written about his exciting life. I absorbed salty energy reading and hearing about him. We were fortunate to have a cottage at Wrightsville Beach, and we always had boats. We had one of the first molded plywood boats twelve-feet long with a five HP motor. I was about twelve.

I would leave the house early, armed with a peanut butter and jelly sandwich, a six ounce Coke and one gallon of gas. I would explore deep into the marsh creeks by myself. What fun! Sometimes I got lost, or the tide would begin to fall, and I would have to drag the boat across a sand bar to the safety of deeper water. There was sometimes a fear of being stranded, but that was part of the excitement. When I was a teen my father's employer gave him a twenty three foot Chris Craft as a retirement gift. My brother Laurens and I, and the Woodbury boys would go fifty miles off shore in the little "Dart" looking for fish. Once we were offshore alongside the "Martha Ellens", Captain Eddy was the star, guru fisherman in those days and our engine stopped. Captain Eddy said he would tow us to shore. For once the "Dart" caught considerably more fish than the "Martha Ellens". When we arrived inshore, Captain Eddy refused payment for the tow but his anglers did take the fish we caught as payment!

Why would anyone be so different to want to sail around the world in a small boat? Crazy? Maybe. In my business as a counselor, I often get the question: "Am I crazy?" I find myself telling people my usual answer: "We are all a little crazy." But let's just call it being different and following a dream. This is an account of a year-long exciting 12,000-mile voyage with my teenaged son, Henry, Jr., twenty years ago.

Sit back and enjoy our memories of that year.

ANNAPOLIS

For years, I had been an interested armchair reader of single-handed voyages. One in particular Francis Stokes sailed around the world in the single handed race in a Valiant 40. He came in second. He seemed like a really nice trustworthy person. He was tall, thin, quiet and confident. After his voyage he had become a yacht broker in Annapolis. I called him in February and told him I was interested in buying a boat and what I wanted to do with it. He asked me to come up to Annapolis to talk and look around the hundreds of boats.

I persuaded Henry, Jr., to go with me. He was seventeen and more interested in his girlfriend Suzanne, the golf team, and graduating from high school. He wanted to do this year-long trip but it was up to Dad to plan and organize. We met Francis and spent much of the day with him. We must have impressed him because he invited us to be his guest at the Slocum Society 25th Annual banquet at the Civic Center that night for cruising people. There were about two hundred people there. We sat at the VIP table with our broker Francis and his wife. He turned out to be one of the speakers and spoke about his solo voyage. He showed slides of surfing on twenty foot waves in the Southern Ocean. Another man, Marvin Creamer a geography professor at an Ivy League College sat next to me with his wife.

Marvin was amazing. I had read his book about sailing around the world with two other men in a thirty eight foot steel boat. The amazing thing about the voyage is they used no navigation devices, no compass, sextant or watch! His hobby was researching ancient sailors and tribes who ventured out to explore new lands. He decided they had to use the stars. He tested his theory by sailing to Bermuda in his thirty two foot sloop. I think he made a crossing, too. Then he had a thirty eight foot steel cutter boat built, which he sailed around the world without even a watch. What an incredible feat!

A third man at our table with his wife was a man from England who made a movie of his voyage across the Atlantic as captain of a wooden replica of a fifteenth-century caraval, which is like the boats Columbus sailed.

What awesome company we were in! We watched some of the Englishman's movie and he narrated. What an incredible evening. I realized these men were not bigger than life, but regular guys, educated, who had a need to stretch themselves beyond where most people would dare to go.

There is a part of me that does not want to do everything like everyone else. There is no adventure in that. These people were all individuals, refreshingly honest, secure and confident, what an experience!

I had some apprehension about our planned voyage. Henry's mother had her fears. What a perfect opportunity to get an expert opinion. So I asked this Ivy League sailor, geography educator, what he thought about our planned trip. He said most kids coming out of high school are not mature enough for college. He said another year and one at sea would be the greatest gift I could give my son. He said "your son will grow and you will grow as father and son together." Well, that did it! Any doubts I had were gone.

We looked at sailboats with our hero/broker Francis. One was a Rival 41, a beautiful English boat. He liked the Rival and said they were strong blue water boats. However, this one was about $130,000, much over our budget.

We looked at some other boats. We looked at Valiant that the broker liked, but it was too expensive, and we could not find anything suitable. Most boats are production boats, they are built with thin skins and light rigging for in-shore or coastal sailing. You do not want to cross oceans in a day sailer. So, with hundreds of boats, our choices were few in Annapolis.

On the drive home from Annapolis to Charlotte, we talked boats. We both liked the Rival 41 and decided to find one in England since that is where they were built. Before leaving Annapolis, we found a British yachting magazine and browsed on the way home. I wanted Henry to be a big part of the planning process. I was learning; I wanted him to experience the excitement of learning and making adult decisions.

We found an English yacht broker in the back want ad section of this yachting magazine. Several days after the Annapolis trip I called this broker. He was a delightful man, very intelligent and polite and proper as you might expect. He won my confidence immediately because of his impeccable English and the fact that he was a sailor. Everything seemed to be falling into place. He said he had bought and sold six or eight Rivals and he loved them. He had sailed on one and was impressed. The broker said he would look around and call me back. A few days later he called back. He had found three used Rival 41's. Two were more than I could afford. The price was right on one located in Gandia, Spain. But why was it lower than the rest? He had some conversations with the owner. The boat was twelve years old. The owner bought the boat with the idea of taking his wife around the world, but his wife had been in an accident and permanently injured her back and was unable to live on a boat much less cross oceans. The broker said he had to go to Spain the following week and could meet me in Gandia. Well now it was time to put up or shut up. I felt anxious and alone. Was this the right thing to do?

The following week, I left Charlotte, flew to New York, and caught a late night Iberia flight to Valencia. I was the only English-speaking person on the plane.

GANDIA

I arrived in Valencia early in the morning with three hours sleep, rented a car and drove about sixty miles south on a scenic highway in rural mid-south Spain. Gandia is a small coastal town, probably 15,000 people. Small mountains rise up from the sea. The marina was nice by Spanish standards--typical concrete quay or wharf, no pilings. Drop the anchor out about 100 feet and back into the quay or stern anchor out and bow tied to the quay. A protective breakwater was three hundred yards away, with a small opening to the Mediterranean. TAIS was laying bow to the quay with the broker and Nigel, the owner, aboard. The broker had broken his leg and was on crutches and cast so he stayed in the cockpit while Nigel showed me around the boat. Nigel is a big but fit appearing man, about six foot three and two hundred twenty pounds. He was serious, not much small talk. Nigel was hard, with working-man hands, cut and callused from years of diesel mechanics. He answered my questions, and tried to raise the price. He knew I had spent a lot of money to fly across the Atlantic to get there. I didn't like this but it was a tip into his personality and who I would be dealing with.

Negotiating the boat deal with Nigel was a memorable experience in a negative way. Nigel had owned a small fleet of six-diesel tour buses. He did everything from driving the buses to managing the business. In addition, he did all of the mechanics, with even pulling and completely rebuilding engines. I was impressed with this because he had completely rebuilt the fifty horsepower British Lister diesel in TAIS. I knew he had done a thorough job as he was putting his life (and his wife's) on the line.

There were things I did not like about TAIS. The interior was only partially finished at the factory. The floor was ugly, just unfinished boards, old, dirty and worn. TAIS had good, deep bilges. They were clean and would make good storage. Bilges are the coolest place on the boat. On TAIS the bilges were actually underneath or below the water line, but not wet.

Nigel arranged for a survey the next day. The broker agreed to stay another day. We motored down the coast about ten miles to an anchored marine railway. We pulled TAIS out of the water and examined her underside. I was not impressed with the surveyor, who could have been a friend of Nigel's, as he was English. I found a number of blisters in the gel-coat underneath. Gel coat is the colored outer skin on a fiberglass boat. The surveyor missed them. Blisters can be very serious and can cost thousands of dollars to repair. I have seen boats sitting on dry land for months draped in plastic shroud trying to dry out the bottom. The blisters pop and seawater enters the fiberglass matting under the hard gel coat. These blisters have to be dug out, the bottom sanded to the mat, dried out-- and a special sealant is applied to keep the water out. Then the bottom is repainted. The surveyor made light of this, as did Nigel.

The surveyor found the engine and mechanical parts of the boat in excellent condition. I was happy about this because mechanics was my and Henry Jr's weakest parts.

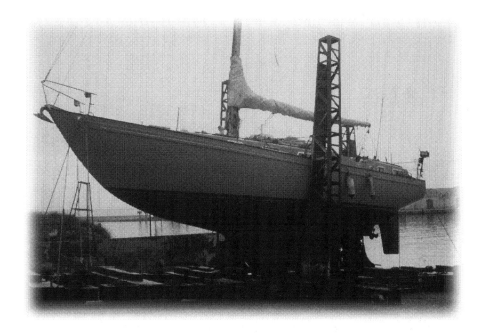

TAIS was being surveyed. I fell in love. This is why boats are named after women.

TAIS stern view.

Galley, gimbled stove, sides on counters.

Navigation station, electrical controls.

Sails were good, rigging sound, as was the hull.

After the surveyor left and we came back to Gandia, the broker initiated the negotiations. I wanted a reduction in price because I felt like the interior had been misrepresented and I was concerned about the blisters. Nigel refused.

The broker asked me to go to the clubhouse while he talked with Nigel. I went to the clubhouse and called my good friend Gene in Wilmington. Gene is in the insurance business and is a boat person and most of all trusted friend.

Gene's advice was if you don't like her, let her go. In fact, Gene said, "Boats are like women. You can always find another one." I felt better after talking with Gene.

I thought about letting her go. She was less than the other Rivals. The broker said if she were pristine she would be worth another $50,000. This sobered me up. I realized I was getting a world class blue water sloop at a really good price and a new engine. The broker talked Nigel down $5,000, and we had a deal. Nigel was not very happy but the deal was closed. We signed papers and I paid him. I gave Nigel some money for next month's rent on the boat slip and told him I would be back in thirty days with my son. I made a written inventory of what was on board and what was needed. I had a lot of gear to buy and ship over in thirty days. The next day I drove back to Valencia and flew home to Charlotte excited about our new home. I showed pictures of TAIS to Henry; she looked more beautiful and Henry loved her.

When I got back to Charlotte, I began research on purchasing gear for TAIS. I'm not going to bore you with all the details, but some of the things I ordered were a pair of Fugicon binoculars. They were five hundred dollars with an excellent compass built in for taking bearings. I knew this would be an important purchase. It turned out to be worth its weight in gold.

Weems and Plathe makes a fine sextant, but just too expensive for me. I settled on an Astro, a less expensive Japanese sextant but with good optics. Cost around four hundred dollars. I also bought a small

Davis plastic sextant for around fifty dollars to put in the grab bag. A grab bag is a canvas bag (in our case) stocked with essentials for survival in case we had to abandon ship and get in the life raft. One sailor said the greatest invention in boating the last fifty years was the Ziploc bag. We bought Ziplocs of all sizes. Great for perishables like flour products or things that mold or mildew on the water. The grab bag contained bottles of distilled water plus a small reverse osmosis hand held pump. This could make about one pint of fresh water from sea water in an hour. Other items were flashlight with extra batteries. All this stuff we put in Ziploc bags. We added some gloves and hand line with hooks and a couple of jigs to catch fish. A Jim Bowie-type knife in holster. Suntan oil, sun screen, two hats, first aid kit, a flare gun with the extra flares, a copy of a chart of the southern Atlantic Ocean, couple Pocket books to read, pen, pencil, memo pads, a couple of life jackets, some extra light line. I also had to buy more gear for TAIS.

- A small Honda generator to power the TV and electric drill
- A thirteen inch black and white TV with VHS
- A twelve gauge shotgun with box of buckshot
- Various cushions and pillows
- Toiletries, soap (Dawn dish soap will lather in salt water)
- Pots and pans
- A ten inch pressure cooker that was a God send
- Foul weather gear
- Boat shoes, gloves, extra bathing suits and t-shirts
- A sun shower, another valuable, and salt water soap
- A 6.0 Penn Reel packed with thirty pound test mono to mount on stern stanchion
- Various feathers, leader wire, jigs, gloves, gaff for fishing

We called various air freight companies and found one that would ship a crate to Valencia, Spain for us. They reserved an open, wooden crate in a corner for us. The crate ended up being a five-foot cube. We made several trips, filling up the cube with our new gear. We shipped this to TAIS care of Henry Wright at Valencia for pick up.

Two weeks later, Henry Sr and Henry Jr were in the air. It was the day after Henry's high school graduation. The flight, like my previous one a month ago was all night on Iberia. Henry brushed up on his Spanish as no one spoke English. Henry became quite good with the Spanish language. I was very proud of him. I am glad, because it was important to me for him to feel like it was his show, too, and not just Dad's. The previous summer Henry spent two months with a Spanish family. He really became fluent because his Spanish family spoke no English. They had a couple of kids and they all learned Spanish and English together. Henry went everywhere they went.

We arrived Valencia early morning with great clapping and cheering as if all the passengers had been holding their breath for hours. We were tired but excited about finally doing what we had dreamed about, my dream for years, Henry's for months. You know, talking about doing something life changing is one thing. Doing it is a whole different challenge. We had made a commitment to be together for a year, sail the Mediterranean, make a crossing, see the Caribbean, and sail home to Wrightsville Beach, NC. Were we crazy or what? Some thought we were. Henry's mother was terrified. "Suppose something happens? You can't take my son."

I pointed out the familiar scenery to Henry and we finally arrived in Gandia where we found TAIS at the dock where I had left her. I was excited and so hoped Henry would like his new home, he did too and he loved TAIS! We called Nigel and told him we had arrived. When he came to open the boat, he was a different person, not angry at all. I guess glad to have his money. He surprised us by inviting us to dinner at his home that night.

Nigel picked us up late afternoon and drove us up the lush mountainside to his home. His home was small, 1,200 square feet Typical Mediterranean; white stucco, terracotta tile roof, lots of open windows, no glass and marble floor. Nigel's wife was nice and quiet and we could tell he was the decision maker in the family. He also did the cooking. Paella was his specialty and it was delicious! A cheap Rose wine in a carton accompanied the paella. Cheap in this case does not mean bad because our first introduction to box wine was quite good. Nigel and his wife remembered hauling TAIS out of the water in Crete. They spent almost a year getting her ready for sea duty, their journey that never happened. He completely overhauled the engine, that part of the visit was sad. Nigel however, seemed happy to see his beloved TAIS going to sea even if he could not be a part of it.

Later, we unloaded the car and put our belongings on board, took a shower at the marina club house. We smelled the soon to be familiar smell of the black Spanish soap cleansing with an antiseptic odor.

Nigel agreed to spend some time with us. He did, couple of hours here and there for four to five days. We wanted to learn as much as we could about TAIS while Nigel was around to answer questions. He showed us how to work the sat nav, electrical system and the engine. We went for a sail. He taught Henry about the foredeck and how to "hank" on sails. We went shopping and bought the two best (but not good enough) deep cycle batteries in Gandia. The original ones were dead.

We decided we could navigate up the coast some sixty miles to Valencia to pick up the crate.

The day before we spent all day on our stomachs, cleaning out the two sixty-gallon stainless steel water tanks. We cleaned through a fifteen inch inspection plate on each tank with Clorox and rinsed and pumped out over and over until they were spotless. The water in Gandia was good but we put a little Clorox, half teaspoon to five gallons. A hand pump in the galley was our only means of running water. We didn't care.

The next day we cast off the bow line backed down to the stern anchor. Hoisted it aboard and motored through the entrance into the Mediterranean, just the two of us. We were so excited. We sailed and motored all night. Early next morning we heard a loud engine noise out of sight but going the same direction. It sounded like racing engines but not revving up high RPMs.

We made Valencia landfall and entered the entrance. All of the boats ahead were going on the wrong side of the buoys. We followed them and later found out the Spanish system was opposite of ours. We found a marina owned by the Governor. It was new, just like in the States with a floating dock!! We eased up to a space and secured dock lines. Ten feet away from us was an incredible racing machine about thirty feet long, very narrow cigarette with three huge V-8 inboards decked over with room for three to four people to squeeze in a tiny cockpit. We had to stand with a curved padded back rest. It had belts to fasten if you wanted.

We had just arrived when the captain spoke to us and cranked her up. Well, it sounded like an explosion! It was so loud. I recognized the sound from earlier. He had just arrived, too!

This man, Dick Thompson, a delivery captain from Fort Lauderdale, was delivering this cigarette to Prince Ranier's daughter who liked speed. This guy was big, six foot three, two hundred twenty pounds, blond curly hair, tanned. He looked like a Fort Lauderdale lifeguard, really good-looking man. He was funny and entertaining and just loved seeing two fellow Americans. He told us about the buoys and said the Spanish did everything "ass backward." He didn't like them much. This should have been a clue.

He said he was invited to a big party across the bay and would we like to come. We said yes. Later in the afternoon he said we would take the Cigarette over. He apologized because one engine was not working. The two that did, however, pinned our ears and eyes back like sticking your head out of a car window doing sixty. That was the fastest I've ever been on the water.

The party was like you see in old Mexican fiesta. One long table one hundred fifty foot long with couples of all ages. Our captain started drinking wine and being funny. We ate several courses, drank more wine and I think sangria. The party got louder. The captain got louder. People started dancing to the band. The women all dressed up. Colorful, until the captain decides to dance and put the make on someone's wife. A fight started but we broke it up and the captain apologized. A little later we look over and the captain is taking his clothes off in front of one hundred fifty people, it doesn't bother him. He dives in the pool screaming like a crazy person. Henry and I decided our good captain had had enough partying! We finally got him out of there without getting in a Spanish jail. The trip back to the marina was slow this time. The characters you meet on the water. Some people when they drink turn into nightmares. The next day we rented a small car and drove around Valencia sight-seeing with a brochure as guide. We passed the train station. You wouldn't think much about a train station, but this one was not only big but the busiest architecture I have ever seen, overkill. Well guess who designed it? A man named Antoni Gaudi. Every time someone says something is "gaudy," I think of this terminal. Nearby was a Chinese restaurant. The sign just said, "Chino." We had a delicious meal. The rest of the trip we would ponder what to eat, the other might say, "Chino!"

Our crate had arrived. We could see it in the back of the freight office. The boss Alejandro, a nasty little Spanish man, didn't like us much. He said the crate was not there. We could see it! We decided to leave and talk about what to do.

On the loading dock a man walks up and tells Henry in Spanish to hire a pickup truck to meet at the loading dock at noon. He could arrange for the truck. For this he wanted twenty five dollars. He said to give the guard at the gate fifty dollars for Alejandro. We were not used to bribery. But that was the way in Spain.

We spent the night downtown in a hotel hoping this caper would work out. We were tired that night and went to sleep early. The hotel was not a fleabag but was not in the best area, we were on the fourth floor. Suddenly we heard loud screeching car noises. We looked out the window, then raised the window to see a taxi come into the intersection and stop. A passenger was pulled out by four young punks with four foot two by four boards. They began beating the man until he fell to the pavement. They took turns and sometimes all beat him at once. I called to the desk and told them to call the police. We yelled out the window, "Stop! Stop!" The punks finally got tired of this madness, stopped hitting the man, quickly got in their car and scratched away yelling I don't know what, as they left.

The victim lay there. The cab driver came back and put the guy in his taxi and left. I hope to go to the hospital. Henry had never experienced anything quite like this. He was visibly upset. So was I. The adrenaline had been pumping. We were both shaking and of course wide awake now.

The police never came but we couldn't afford to get too involved being in a foreign country. All cities have their gangs and thugs. This put a memorably black mark on an ancient city.

The air pollution in Valencia was very bad, small particles seemed to always be in the outside air. It was so bad Henry could not wear his contacts.

The next morning we went to the freight warehouse to do battle with Alejandro, the little beast. He actually was pleasant; I supposed it was because he knew he was getting his bribe money. The pickup truck arrived. It was smaller than anything I had ever seen in the states. When Alejandro and crew slid the crate into the bed with about 1 inch to spare, Henry and I crammed in the front seat with the driver. The front wheels actually came off the pavement when he started. We hoped the driver knew what he was doing!

When we started moving, he eased the tiny truck up to the guard-house, paid the guard the bribe money, and we looked at each other with a sigh of relief as we headed to the marina and TAIS.

The marina, being a government facility, was protected by an armed guard from Franco's red berets. The guard was a soldier with uniform, boots, and an automatic rifle at the ready. Henry and I unloaded the crate at the marina entrance and the driver left. We opened TAIS and came back down the dock with a screwdriver and hammer to open the crate. The guard seemed interested and I wondered out loud to Henry what we were going to do about the shotgun and shells. I thought it is surely against the law to bring firearms into the country. We made a plan! We started taking our cushions and gear out, making numerous trips back and forth from the crate down the dock to TAIS and back. We saw the gun and shells. Henry was to engage the soldier in conversation; being sure the man's back was turned to the crate, while I pulled out the shotgun and shells and hurried down the dock to TAIS. The plan worked to perfection partly, I expect, because the soldier was bored with the crate by now, and partly because Henry did a great job of distracting him. The guard said he would dispose of the empty crate for us.

Our friendly captain who got so drunk and obnoxious at the party earlier had already left to deliver the cigarette to the princess in Monaco.

We were happy to have our new gear aboard and happy to leave Valencia as well.

We had a glorious all night sail down the rocky Spanish Coast under full main and Genoa sail. The sea was calm, but there was enough wind to push us along. I took a great photo of the full Moon and a lighthouse. We talked about our trip to Valencia and how fortunate we were to be able to be on this adventure.

Henry slept some. I slept some, but not much because I felt so excited. We were tired when we arrived at Gandia. Gandia was a small coastal town about eighty miles south of Valencia. We doused the sails, cranked the engine, and motored through the breakwater to our dock space. We let out the stern forty five pound plow CQR anchor and put the bow up against the concrete quay.

We slept for a few hours, then got up and began storing gear. We made a list of where we put things. Although the boat is small, it is incredible how easy it is to lose things. With my ADD, this was an even bigger problem.

Along the coastal highway in Gandia are miles of vegetable farms. The soil must be rich as gold because the fruit and vegetables are the most delicious I have ever tasted. We have Valencia oranges in the USA and I always wondered where they came from.

Two restaurants in Gandia stand out in my memory. The first was small, inexpensive and good. Like most Spanish restaurants, there was no atmosphere, just plain simple chairs, tables and neon lights. The waiter looked exactly like Ernest Borgnine - an ugly man but with a face of great character and Ernest is married to Ethel Merman, the great song and dance lady still working at ninety. This waiter, the only one, we called Earnest. I had to ask him if he knew of Borgnine. He only spoke Spanish so we didn't get very far with that conversation. Earnest, however, made us the best salads with incredible vine ripe tomatoes and greens and green peppers. Green peppers have always given me indigestion, not these. It must have been the soil or the fact they were fresh, locally grown and probably organic.

The second memorable restaurant in Gandia was Loepu, more expensive and the best in Gandia. Troubadours walked around the restaurants main dining room playing and stopping at tables. There was a huge middle aged man at a table with several other men. He was boisterous, but not obnoxious and actually friendly. He could see we were Americans. Henry used his rudimentary Spanish to converse across the room to his nearby table. I asked Henry to ask him what to order. He said, "The menu." Well, we didn't know exactly what that meant, but the waiter did. For the next hour he brought us course after course. We ate fresh caught octopus and squid raw and cooked. The cooked squid was delicious, as were most of the other dishes. The big guy was enjoying watching us trying to eat this twenty course meal. His laughter could be heard all over the restaurant. He invited us over to his table afterwards, for some fine wine and a fine cigar. I don't smoke and neither does Henry but we were not going to refuse the local godfather. We did the best we could, but we both got dizzy and staggered out into the street some time later with our half smoked cigars.

One of my goals for this trip was to educate and instill into my son, at least some of my appreciation for boating, sailing and sea life. I had had considerable experience in the navy as a Radar man and Navigator, plus having owned small craft and fishing off the North Carolina Coast my entire life. I had, and still have, profound respect for the unforgiving fierceness of the ocean, as well as its serenity, the closeness to God I feel there, and the primitive power of commanding a vessel by manipulating a huge canvas sail to harness the wind. Neptune had his chariot pulled by dolphins. At sea I can sometimes feel an invisible force pulling my "chariot". Sailing, feeling the power of the wind, the sea and the sail is a real honest to goodness power trip.

I wanted my son Henry to fully appreciate all of this power and beauty, the experience of God's presence on the sea. But teenagers are not always into the Zen of living.

Another reason for my wanting Henry to be a competent sailor was for our safety and survival. If something terrible happened to me, he would have to get us or at least himself safely to land.

I taught him first from a globe latitude and longitude. Then he learned a segment of the globe on a nautical chart. He learned how to read a chart and we studied lots of them. I would put a dot on a chart and ask Henry to tell me the latitude and longitude, or I would give him the latitude and longitude then ask him to plot the position on the chart. We studied dead reckoning, which is how to take bearings on light houses, rocks, mountains and plot them on the chart. We talked about how a change of course projected. When the trip is actually taken, this course is usually amended many times, but it is a plan to follow. Just as in life, we need some sense of where we're going and set a course to get there, even though we often amend it, depending on the circumstances and unexpected situations.

Henry is smarter than I am. He learned fast, and thank God, he will tell me the truth if he does not know something. I've known some people who just will not admit to not knowing something. They are of no use then, when the chips are down.

I learned the truth about people not telling the truth in the wonderful training I received in the Navy. We would train and practice, train and practice, until we could do whatever it was in our sleep. It became a muscle memory. It showed right away if someone wasn't pulling their weight.

Henry was never subjected to that kind of discipline. His father was much easier on him. Fortunately, Henry was always a very self disciplined person, I always admired him for that and I do hope that I instilled some of that self discipline in him. He needed this incredible discipline to finish this adventure safely. Henry had to take orders from the Captain, sometimes without question or hesitation; our lives would depend on it!

I wanted Henry to be able to marvel at an incredibly large orange Moon behind an ancient lighthouse in Spain, to really be present in the moment of this site in the quiet night. I wanted us to talk about it, to appreciate a once in a lifetime sight most others will never see. I didn't want Henry to give these sights a passing glance. This is not really seeing. How can you love something or somebody if you cannot truly see them? I wanted him to learn this truth, too.

TAIS

We had a pretty good inventory of sails, one main sail with three sets of reef points. Reef points are the little pieces of line about twelve inches long attached in a straight line about one third of the way up the main sail, then another set another one third up to give a two reef system. You've probably noticed these little lines about pencil thickness hanging on either side of mainsails as you pass a sailboat.

If the wind is too strong, then you put one or two reefs on the main to make it shorter. In order to do this, you have to round, or turn the boat up facing into the wind, drop the main down to where the first reef points are aligned with the boom. There is a grommet to secure the sail to the mast where the mast and boom connect behind or aligned with the reef points. There is another grommet at the aft end of the boom that is attached to a line at the end of the boom. Then the flagging, flapping loose sail is gathered on top of the boom and each reef point (maybe eight) are tied around the loose sail to make it tight with a reef knot or square knot. Now what we have is shortened sail.

Shortening (or reefing) a sail is done for several reasons.

Every boat has a maximum given hull speed that is determined by the boat architect, who has a formula based on length, width, hull and bottom design and weight. Our ideal hull speed was a little over seven knots. Prudent sailors try to keep their boat close to hull speed. A boat can be overpowered by wind and waves to the point of capsizing. The higher the wind and waves, the more sail needs to be reefed or shortened.

We practiced reefing in the calm waters of the Mediterranean Sea. One thing, as I mentioned earlier, the navy taught me is that practice makes perfect. I knew we would encounter bad weather, so I wanted to be very sure we knew how to do this maneuver so well it became second nature to us. It takes real team work, without yelling and making mistakes. Henry, like most teens, didn't see the value of this practice in calm weather. At sea, much later, he realized its utmost importance!

TAIS was forty one foot long, sloop rigged, with a 12.3 beam, five foot eleven draft. 22,000 lbs. Rival 41 center cockpit. The aft cabin with its own toilet compartment (head) is reached from its own companionway in the cockpit or via a walkway from the salon. Aft of a small walkway is a custom queen sized berth, wall to wall. This proved invaluable underway in a rolling sea because the person could lay spread eagle and sleep.

The engine room was easily accessible in the passageway. Foreword of the main ladder from the cockpit is the salon. The navigation station is starboard, the galley port. Foreword of the galley is the leather bunk with a settee that drops to a double bed. Opposite of the settee is a leather sofa, then foreword a head to port, and closet is starboard. Foreword another bulkhead and the foreword cabin. This was Henry Jr's domain with two large vee births. Foreword into the bow is an anchor chain locker.

Fresh air was always available through two large hatches, one foreword, one after over the aft cabin, plus two smaller hatches amidship. We rigged a wind scoop for each hatch plus the main hatch. The wind scoop is a piece of canvas about four feet long and the width, or the diameter of the hatch is cut and stitched onto a wooden dowell at the top, to form a bridle. The bridle is then attached to a halyard or boom overhead. The bottom of the scoop has three grommets with small nylon lines. These lines are fastened to eye hooks around the base of the hatch. When in place, these scoops catch the wind and sails it right down below. We were seldom too hot because of this constant, natural breeze in the cabin.

MALLORCA TO CORFU

Palma de Mallorca is a pretty, old city on the island of Mallorca. Mallorca is a playground for the rich. On our arrival we anchored in a bay. There was crystal clear water underneath us, beautiful mountains all around us. It was the kind of place you want to stay awhile. I woke up early, as usual, fixed my coffee and went up on deck. Henry usually slept an hour or two longer. While I was enjoying the sunrise, sipping my brew, I heard a swishing sound. I turned around in time to see a twenty-something naked woman windsurfing twenty feet behind TAIS. I couldn't wait to tell Henry. He was dismayed to have missed the girl. He got his chance, though. Many women there were topless or naked altogether, around the water. This was one of many exciting and beautiful cities we would visit during the next year.

A good life raft is a must for deep water cruising. Nigel told us the four man Avon raft was newly packed. We by now learned to take whatever he said with a grain of salt. This life raft is packed inside a plastic canister and mounted on a cradle on top of the cabin just behind the mast, under the boom. It is self inflating. When working properly, it can be opened several ways. A Painter, a twenty foot piece of line can be yanked, breaking the watertight seal and the raft pops out as it is inflating. Or, if the boat were to turn over or sink, the water pressure would trigger the case to open and the inflated raft would float to the surface.

We asked around Mallorca and found an old German sea caption licensed to repack rafts. We called him. Fortunately, he spoke English although with a thick German accent. He agreed to look at the TAIS' raft. We removed the raft from the deckhouse and carried it to a taxi. When we arrived at the shop, we were met by a huge man with a stern "don't be close" look. He soon warmed up to us when he saw how desperately we needed his help. He said he was envious of our touring, but that his life at sea had ended. His hands were huge, with fingers the size of American quarters. He had a very large head, with white hair protruding from underneath his Greek captain's hat. He grabbed the canister like it was a lunch pail and took it into his shop. He popped the canister open and we heard the hissing of the air canister going off in the orange square rubber raft. It may have been four or five feet square, hardly big enough for two people, much less four.

We were serious because we knew we might have to spend some time in this thing at sea, possibly rough seas. The old German captain led a discussion about what we needed to buy for the raft:

- Flashlight with extra batteries
- Ziploc bags
- Good hand line for fishing with hooks and feather jigs
- Cotton work gloves, sunscreen
- A mirror, pencil and paper
- Distilled water
- First aid kit and knife
- Extra shirts in Ziploc bag

He said for us to come back in two days. We took a taxi to downtown Palma where we found a large department store that carried most of the items we needed.

We went back to the captain's shop as scheduled. He seemed to like us and probably thought we needed as much advice as he could give. Henry and I both got in the inflated raft to get a feel of what it might be like should we be in a predicament where we would have to be in it longer than a few minutes. The feeling was fear; it was the thought of depending on this tiny rubber raft for survival. It was very small, but we thought three could survive if we had to.

It was a pretty cool raft. It had an enclosed canopy with a window and a zippered door. It had side curtains that went about four feet under water and filled with water for balance at sea. We packed all of our stuff in Ziploc bags and watched the old captain carefully repack it all in our raft. We paid him, thanked him and felt secure about our newly and properly packed raft.

I splurged on a premium first aid kit. It was the size of a large tackle box and opened out six tiers with a little of everything. Earlier, I had bought a great book written by a surgeon sailor, who had sailed around the world. He explained in detail how to cut off a leg or arm and how to put a dislocated shoulder back in place by tying a weight on the arm and lying on a bunk and dropping the weight off the bunk toward the floor, yanking the arm away from the shoulder socket and allowing it relocate itself in the socket. He said we would definitely need some Zylocaine or morphine and a syringe. We went to a drug store in Palma and asked to speak to the owner. We showed him a picture of TAIS. Henry explained about our voyage. We were lucky and walked out of the drug store with a bottle of Novocain and six syringes. We hoped we would never have to use them.

Docking a sailboat the size of TAIS can always be challenging. One of the wildest docking maneuvers happened when we were walking the dock in Palma de Mallorca. We were looking for used charts to buy. Nigel had told us charts to anywhere were available in Palma. Palma de Mallorca is a pretty big, old, and beautiful city with hundreds of yachts, but no charts. We learned to be thankful when you could buy a chart at any West Marine store in the United States. In Palma, there were none. I told Henry we would put on our sales hats. He would take one pier, I would take another; knocking on hulls or if we saw someone aboard, we asked if they had any charts to sell. We did pretty well, actually. We were given or paid for six charts, enough to get us to Greece and up the coast of Italy. They were beautiful charts, in Spanish or Italian.

There is a certain etiquette around docks. If you are on a pier or quay and a boat comes up to dock, the neighborly thing to do is handle the lines for the captain. We saw a beautiful forty foot Spanish cabin cruiser bearing down on us. The captain was a very distinguished looking man, tall, white haired, with a mustache, about fifty-ish. He was at the wheel. His wife, of similar age, was on the foredeck handling the anchor. In the Mediterranean, mooring is bow anchored and stern tied to the quay. No poles were allowed. This Spanish couple was about fifty yards away and coming in at ten knots. I said, "Henry, we'd better get out of the way, he's going to ram the quay." At the precise moment, the captain yells something in Spanish and his wife cuts loose the anchor which is secured by a long chain. Imagine the noise made from the heavy chain flying out of the chain locker through the deck plate through the chocks. About forty two feet from the cement quay, the anchor grabbed bottom and flipped the boat around. The captain by then was in the cockpit two feet away and nonchalantly handed me a stern line and said "Gracias". We were stunned and amazed at the man's ability to maneuver his yacht with an anchor. When we asked him about it, he said it was easy. We said he and his wife must have practiced this anchor/docking maneuver hundreds of times. He was flattered by our interest and gave us a chart. It is amazing how most people are nice if you are nice first. A smile, a handshake, a look in the eye with no anger, works wonders in befriending people. My father was a master at this ability, and I had learned it by osmosis. Henry has this trait, in befriending, as do many of my family members, a gift for which we are all grateful.

We departed Palma de Mallorca early in the morning en route to the south tip of Sardinia, two hundred fifty miles east of Palma. El Toro Light was our next way point. Our ultimate destination Corfu, Greece, was about five hundred miles east. We had to sail around the southern tip of Sardinia, along the northern coast of Sicily, through the strait of Messina, down the south coast of Italy, across the Ionian Sea to Corfu! I had heard Corfu was great. I had been to most of the other more popular Greek Islands on a cruise ship, a very different experience from having your own boat and going where you want to go, when you want to go.

This first leg was really our first open water trip. At this point we were getting pretty comfortable with TAIS, but we were still green. If she could have talked she would probably have said "It will be a miracle if these two city boys can get me home in one piece." One beautiful thing about this experience was the joy and excitement of learning, not learning at home in a safe place, but learning on the job. This job was survival and getting from point A and point B safely.

We mostly motored this leg. Occasionally a whisper of air would allow us to sail. Our satellite navigation (Sat Nav) showed us about fifteen miles from El Toro Light. The night was black, no moon, no stars, and a fog settling in. We slowed to a snail's pace, on course to our way point. I took several more fixes on the Sat Nav. The last one showed El Toro one mile ahead. Still, we saw nothing. No sails were up; we were motoring as slow as we could. Henry suddenly said, "What is that?" and pointed almost straight above us. I looked up thinking a star had broken through the cloud cover. It was blinking, but not like a star, more like a beacon! I said, "Henry, that's El Toro!" Simultaneously, the dark outline of a mountain appeared dead ahead, right on top of us! I spun the wheel hard to the right and away, to allow El Toro to pass down our port side. This scared the "bejesus" out of both of us. Here we were on our first two hundred mile sail, and I almost put TAIS on the rocks! Hitting a mountain no less. I was scared to know what TAIS was thinking, "Are these guys going to learn?" I double checked the chart, it just showed a light. El Toro was well named and an experience well learned.

TAIS's log shows us July 28, 1986, at 0130 hours passing the southern tip of Sardinia, changing course to 098 degrees, light off Palermo 220 mi. We were running under power on "port tank" wind from the north at five knots. TAIS was not a light air boat and five knots of wind was not enough to sail. We were eager to sail, though, so at 0900 we shut off the engine, hoisted the main and hoisted the light Genoa. The wind had picked up to ten knots. An hour later the wind died (1000), so we dropped sail and were again under power. Sail boats are much more comfortable under sail than under power. Under power, a heavy, lead filled six foot keel and fifty foot mast, the boat is like a pendulum and will roll side to side. If you are under power alone and there are waves, the rolling back and forth can be almost unbearable. Rarely is the sea just totally dead calm with no swell.

On this day, to dampen the roll, we hoisted the main and sheeted it tight. This helped.

TAIS log:On Tue. July 29 at 11:00 am, we passed Palermo Light, our waypoint. We changed course to 110 degrees 42 mi headed to Milazzo, Sicily. At 1900 hours, we motored in to Milazzo harbor, following a ferry boat.

At this point, we had already broken a cardinal rule: Don't enter a strange or foreign port at night.

One of the questions frequently asked me was, "Why didn't you just anchor?" I guess this is a logical question, but in this area of the Mediterranean, there is no bottom to anchor to. Some of the depths in the Med are a half mile deep. We would have had to pull a barge loaded with anchor line just to reach the bottom.

Milazzo is a quaint old seaport. Everything is old in Europe. We looked for a dock or marina where we could tie up and get some sleep. We finally found an ancient quay, so old that it was probably there long before Columbus discovered America. In fact, the whole town was like being in a time warp. The Sicilians seemed more austere than the Italians, although they are only a few short miles apart. I remember my first loaf of Sicilian bread we bought at the bakery. It looked like a dark brown deflated basketball and was hard. We didn't think much of it until we cut a couple slices. The hard crust sealed in the soft core inside. With some fresh butter, this was a wonderful treat. We went back and bought two more loaves, which we enjoyed over the next two days.

An old steel homemade sailboat about thirty five foot long, rusty, and black, was tied up in front of us. The boat had Australia on her stern. She had a plexiglass bubble over the companionway hatch so the captain could see out in foul weather. An old codger appeared on deck. He must have been in his seventies, thin, with a full white beard, a single hander.

I walked over and introduced myself. He had sailed all the way from Australia by himself in this old rust bucket. It looked awful but was apparently quite seaworthy. He said he had encountered days in the Southern ocean when he was under storm sail, with waves crashing all over him and the boat. He was about the "saltiest" man I have ever met. He reminded me of Tristan Jones, who wrote sea stories about sailing alone around the world.

After a good night's sleep, we pulled away from the ancient quay. The old man untied our lines and bade us farewell. After so much motoring, we decided we should top off our tanks; so we began searching for a fuel dock. Unlike the US, where you can get fuel most anywhere, Milazzo was a one fuel pump town. We had to wait in line while half a dozen other boats refueled. While we were refueling, we decided it would be good to change the oil as well. Changing the oil was a real challenge! There was a companionway leading from the main cabin aft to the master stateroom. Midway was a removable door that exposed the engine room, with easy access to the starboard side of the engine. As with cars, when you change the oil in a boat, the filter should be changed too. This is dirty business with a diesel. Henry was changing the oil, as I was fueling. I finished and paid the man because other people were waiting, so I asked Henry to hurry. He quickly finished, and we cranked up and pulled away from the fuel dock, headed out to the open but small turn around basin. About two hundred yards out, I noticed the oil gauge went down to zero. I quickly shut then engine off and ran down below. I saw oil leaking. Henry, in his haste, had cross threaded the new oil filter, and the engine had pumped all six quarts of fresh oil into the bilge. What a mess!

Fortunately, although Milazzo was small, it was a port for ferries going to Palermo, Messina and Italy. These ferries are huge three hundred to five hundred foot long, triple decked, loaded with hundreds of cars and people.

We were dead in the water, unable to start the engine, when we heard a series of deafening "doooooo doooooo doooooo" from a ferry bearing down on us. Small boats, even with the right of way, have to move fast to get out of the way of the big guys or get run over. I ran to the companionway up the ladder, saw the ferry, and yelled at Henry to hank on the Light Genoa fast! Fortunately, he had had some practice by now and got the Genoa up. There was the tiniest bit of breeze; barely enough to fill the sail as we slowly began to move. The ferry passed a few feet behind us. We wondered what else could go wrong. We were soon to find out.

Henry felt bad about the cross threading of the filter. I remember telling him we were still learning how to do this. We screwed the filter on correctly, put in six quarts of new oil, and got underway at 1000 Thurs, July 31, bound for the strait of Messina.

. It was a beautiful day, with light wind, but enough to sail under main and light Genoa. At 1300 hours, we rounded Rasocolomo Point and changed course to one hundred five degrees, headed for our next way point Faro Light, bearing one hundred twenty degrees.

One of the items I splurged on for TAIS was a great pair of binoculars. They were very expensive and had a built in compass. When piloting, part of navigating is taking bearings on visual objects that are on the chart, like buoys, rocks, points of land, even mountains that can be seen for many miles. You see land visually, but you lose sight off and on, so you steer from a course you have drawn on your navigation chart to go from point A to point B. Then you parallel rule to the compass rose and get your course to steer. It is nice to have waypoints, something you can see both on the chart and on land. Going around a point, for example, which requires changing course, you need to know exactly when to change course. Because of our broad visual view it was almost impossible to guess when a light or waypoint reads one hundred twenty degrees; but by looking through these binoculars with the compass, there was a centerline mark that enabled us to get an accurate bearing. When Faro Light, for example, bears one hundred twenty degrees, we could only be in one spot and knew it was time to change course. We would then put the date and time on the chart beside a line drawn from waypoint (Faro Light in this case) across your course line for future reference. Then we could measure how far and what course to take the next waypoint. So we were moving on a chart, a big piece of paper, as well as moving in real life.

In the sail inventory I mentioned the Light Genoa. This sail was brand new and Nigel had told me a number of times it was his pride and joy; and I'm sure it had been painful for him to buy such an expensive sail. This was a Big Genoa you could sheet in tight that came back beyond midship. It was not as light as spinnaker cloth, but much lighter than our other cruising sails. It was good for winds as strong as twelve to fifteen knots.

There were mountains to starboard blocking a wind we did not know about. Messina is the bottom end of a funnel. Across the strait of Messina about one mile lies Italy, with her mountains, and to the right Sicily, with her mountains. This funnel is about twenty miles long to the southern tip of Italy and Sicily. The mouth is about fifteen miles wide and narrows to one mile where we were at the tip.

We were totally unprepared for the huge blast of wind that hit us as we rounded Faro Light and began the entrance to Messina Strait. The wind had been funneling for twenty miles with mountains for sides. Sailing is doing nothing then frantically doing all that has to be done all hell breaks loose. It hit us. To keep from turning over, I let out on the main, headed into the wind some, and yelled at Henry to drop the Genoa. He scampered to the foredeck, but before we could get the sail down, I watched as it shredded into pieces. It was a sickening sight!

Poor TAIS! Nigel, sensing how badly "his" boat was being treated, probably ran off the road in Gandia. We just looked at each other. "We're learning", I kept telling myself and Henry. We put up the working jib and put a reef in the main for a while, until we got further along.

Ridiculous Sicilian swordfish boat.

For some strange reason, swordfish are frequently caught in the Strait of Messina. They are caught in a truly ridiculous manner. Picture a thirty eight foot wooden fishing boat with a twenty foot frame spotting tower above. Protruding outward from the bow is a one hundred foot aluminum, narrow walkway where a man can stand at the end surrounded by aluminum tubing with a harpoon in his hand. This long funny looking pulpit is supported by a number of fine guy wires, or stays, that run from the tower to the sides and the waterline. A sailboat has the right of way over a power vessel, but that doesn't seem to make much difference in Sicily. One of these sword fish boats decided to turn and head in our direction. You may recall if you have ever water skied, that when the boat turns, the skier flies out three to four times as fast as the boat. Well, that's the way this was when the boat turned, the long pulpit came flying at us doing about twenty knots. We were helpless and were about to jam ourselves into the cockpit, when the pulpit contraption missed us by inches. We looked at each other in disbelief. I have often wondered if this was just good seamanship on his part, or if we were just lucky, or both. We took pictures of this unusual boat and moved on.

I told Henry that my mother's favorite place in Sicily was a little town called Tormina. It was not far out of the way, so we decided to sail down the East Coast for a visit. Night came and it was another one without moon or stars. I dislike moving on land or water when you cannot see. The wind died so we cranked up the engine and motored down the coast. The sat nav showed us off Tormina but there was no visibility. We did have a handheld 500,000 candlepower plug-in spot light but it would not penetrate the fog. I said, "Let's give up on this idea and head for open water and Corfu." As we turned, we saw with the light a series of corks floating on the surface as far as the light could penetrate the darkness. We decided to follow the cork line to its end so we could get through, as it was seaward of us. We were trapped in a gigantic fishing net! We moved north about a half mile. No end to the corks. We turned around and motored south along the cork line another half mile. No end. This situation was getting ridiculous and we were getting more and more angry by the minute. Cutting a man's fishing net is probably a serious crime and we didn't want angry Sicilian fishermen chasing us. After several hours of being trapped and seeing no other way out, that's what we decided to do, cut the net to freedom with a very sharp fishing knife we had ready to use. Henry was elected to go overboard. He stood on the transom with knife in his teeth, ready to dive, when two blinding spot lights lit up a twenty five square yard area of water. We saw a fishing boat twenty yards away with four screaming Sicilians shaking their fists at us. We couldn't understand a word they were saying. I held up my hands and motioned my best charade style that all we wanted was a way out. Henry tried talking to them in Spanish. After about fifteen minutes, their anger subsided, and they got the message that we were just two dumb lost Americans who desperately wanted out of the net they had encircled us with. They motioned us to follow them. Not knowing where we were and not knowing what we were doing, our subconscious mind had played tricks on us. We discussed, in our tired frustrated state, what we thought these guys were up to. Did they have guns aboard? Where were they leading us? Communication is a wonderful thing when it's working. The language barrier prevented meaningful communication; and we were left to guess who they were, what they were up to, and where they were leading us. After more than an hour of following these characters we hoped were fishermen, they had stopped. They gestured to us that we were free, chattering all the while and now laughing. Henry shined our spot light on the water and we could see that sure enough, the corks had disappeared. I turned TAIS eastward, stood up on deck, made a formal bow like an opera singer and waved farewell. The fishermen laughed and disappeared into the fog.

We set a course north east towards the Greek island of Corfu, two hundred fifty miles across the Ionian Sea. It was about one am and we were both exhausted. I slept below for three hours then relieved Henry so he could get some sleep. For the next couple of days, the Ionian Sea was as calm as a lake, with slight swells. We motored six knots with main hoisted and sheeted in tight with the boom amidships. These were lazy cruising days.

On Saturday at 20:00 hours we rounded the Paxoi Greece Light following a fishing boat into a small bowl of an anchorage and anchored in fifteen feet of crystal clear water, shut off the engine, cut off the running lights and lit the anchor light atop the mast. We both slept late in this safe little harbor. I always woke up early and had coffee on deck in the cockpit. I couldn't wait to wake Henry to share the beauty of this exquisite little Greek island. In the Med, anchorages are natural and haven't changed for centuries. Unlike the States, there are few buoys, but lots of rocks and natural navigation points. Also, there are no tides; therefore there are no sandbars. This little bay of Paxoi, about the size of two football fields was surrounded by rocks and greens with a narrow opening to let boats in and out.

We had a routine at anchor. We would tie two bumpers horizontally on the portside opposite the cockpit. Outboard of the bumpers we tied a boarding ladder. Then we unroll the deflated Zodiac dingy, unpack the foot pump, and proceed to take turns pumping air to inflate the dingy. When it was full of air we slid the dingy into the water and tie it off. Henry Jr would get in the dingy, bring it around the stern and I would lower the little Yamaha four hp outboard (mounted on the stern rail) down to him. He then placed it on the transom and tightened the clamps. This took some time but time was what we had and no one was in a hurry. In fact, we were really beginning to learn to relax. Anybody who thinks they can totally relax on a week vacation is wrong. Maybe they can relax a bit but it had taken us weeks to relax this much.

At the far end of the little bay of Paxoi is the tiny village of Lakka. We loved this little place. Out of the tourists' way, the people were friendly and there was a wonderful little restaurant on the water. We dingied to Lakka and spent most of the day exploring. The Greek people were so nice and welcoming/open. We spent another night there and left at noon, Wed en route Corfu, twelve mi north.

When we were at anchor near other boats and a new boat came in everybody noticed, looked at the boat and its country of origin flags. Somebody would usually row over, welcome them, invite them over. Sometimes we would invite them over for drinks on TAIS. These people sailed their own boats.

The fact that they were there, proved they knew what they were doing and there is a strange immediate acceptance. It did not seem to be of much importance what kind of boat they called home. It could be a million dollar yacht or a rusty steel ketch like the old salt from Australian called home. His boat was not worth $10,000. Who cared? The old man was charming, hospitable, and very knowledgeable. We really did not see many wealthy people cruising. I guess they were too busy working to make more money or afraid they might be robbed.

The cruising people we met were individuals. They were willing to be different, to go off the accepted path, to take a calculated risk. Most were ordinary, but educated people, following some getaway dream. I believe a person has to appreciate nature and the romantic, adventurous call of the sea, to be willing to sell everything and sail the world. I admire anyone who carves out a portion of their life to do this. The experience and memories are far beyond most people's comprehension. Maybe they are afraid to leave their hot showers and their comfortable lives and Charlotte Observer.

On Sunday, August third we arrived in Corfu at 1500 hours. We anchored downtown under the bastion. Stern anchor, bow to the ancient stone quay. Everything was so old, to us as Americans, in this part of the world.

The Greek language was difficult for us and because they use a different alphabet, the written word was just as hard. Trying to read a road sign or shop sign required some thinking, like going back to fraternity/sorority days with the Greek alphabet. But we managed and became good at charades. We also discovered if we wanted directions, we should not ask anyone over twenty; they didn't speak English. The best communication was with a ten to fifteen year old. They enjoyed conversing because English is now taught in their schools, and they can practice for real.

We located the customs office and had the usual wait. All the countries we visited were different but customs offices and officers were similar. Customs usually includes immigration, but sometimes we had to go to another office, somewhere else in town. Most of these places like Corfu were not using computers. We would have to fill out paperwork, have documents, ie passports, maybe our US driver's license, and vessel documentation. How long would we be there, what was our purpose? Many questions to answer. This process could take two hours to a half day, depending on the country. We realized we take a lot for granted in the U.S.

There was something nostalgic for me about this process. I could imagine Columbus sitting there, being logged into a handwritten ledger, in order to enter Greece.

We were expecting my daughter Virginia and former wife Ginny, our first guests, to arrive on Saturday. They didn't. We later found out they had missed a flight from Athens to Corfu and had had to sleep on the floor in the Athens airport. When they did arrive they were tired. Henry and I were not getting tired of each other, but it was good to have some other loving family around, if just for a visit and we loved having them. It is so much fun seeing the excitement of a new experience in someone else's eyes. Just sharing the togetherness!

Henry and Virginia in Corfu.

While they were there, we rented a car and drove all over Corfu. We saw old churches and olive groves. A thousand year old olive tree would be beside a church or in someone's yard. They were beautiful and felt like sacred ground. Ginny said she felt as if she were back in biblical times. She loved that! We were treated to a beautiful parade downtown. It was celebrating a patron saint. Men, women, and children were all dressed up in beautiful traditional costumes. The most amazing part of the parade was the saint himself, several hundred years old, preserved with his skin intact and clothed with robes and a large pope-like hat, sitting in a chair. He was carried in a phone booth like glass container. The booth had a pole on either side and was carried in the parade on the shoulders of six men. I thought it was morbid but these Greeks seemed to love it.

Walking in downtown Corfu was an adventure. There were good simple restaurants, butcher shops with no refrigeration, live chickens in cages. You could have them killed on the spot and have them dressed, or they could be bought live and you would do your own killing. Four legged animals were hung upside down, skinned with the hooves and feet and some fur left on so customers could identify what kind of animal they wanted to buy. Ginny and Virginia found some beautiful jewelry in a shop there, and bought some clothes as well.

We decided to take Virginia and Ginny sailing on Tuesday. We chose to go back to Paxoi because Henry and I had loved it so much. I have always enjoyed getting out of cities to small islands and towns and countryside. The people are usually more friendly and enjoy helping and haven't been subjected to embarrassing, obnoxious American tourists.

The water was clear in this part of the Med. We dropped a safety line over the stern. This life line was seventy five feet of heavy rope, with knots every few feet and a loop in the end. If someone were to fall overboard it could be difficult to turn the boat around or if you were the only one on deck and fell off you could swim to the life line. Virginia, Henry and Ginny enjoyed being dragged behind the boat on the life line. We never saw a shark in the Med. It is so void of fish that not many sharks could have survived. In the Atlantic I would not have allowed dragging or swimming. A shark could see a swimmer from several hundred feet down and the person wouldn't have a chance if the shark wanted you for dinner.

Paxoi was fun. The little bay was like a big aquarium. We swam there, riding on anchor. I took this opportunity to put on a mask and snorkel and inspect the underwater part of the boat. This inspection included the hull fittings, the rudder, the propeller, the skeg and the keel. I always wanted to inspect my anchor on the bottom so I could sleep well at night, knowing TAIS was not going anywhere. I discovered that, as the captain, always slept lightly, feeling an interesting heightened survival awareness that was acquired. I've been amazed at human survival instincts and how, when we are put in a position to need them, they will appear. Any wind change or position of waves or weather conditions would instinctively awaken this survival mechanism.

The little town of Lattka was a small place to visit, with the good little restaurant on the water. We dingied back to TAIS after dinner, and everybody slept well. There was a little bit of excitement in just dingying back and forth for our guests. It was part of the camping like nature experience and could be exciting if there was wind or waves.

The next day we hoisted anchor, said farewell to our little private anchorage, and sailed back to Corfu. Ginny was impressed with our ability to maintain and command TAIS to do what we wanted. This was a nice compliment because as we had gradually become more proficient at sailing, Henry and I weren't aware of our progress. I realized we were much better than when we'd left Gandia, but far from as good as we needed to be to cross oceans.

Ginny and Virginia stayed a couple more days, then flew back to the States. We hated to see them go, but were ready to move on ourselves.

While we were in Corfu, we took the new light Genoa that got ripped in Messina to a sail maker who restitched it. He did a good job but the sail never regained its original shape.

We also found fresh water for our tanks through the nautical grapevine in Corfu. As I've mentioned, boating people are wonderful at giving newcomers local information. We were told to phone the waterman and make an appointment to take TAIS about five miles to an isolated pier near a small, barren mountain, maybe one thousand feet high. When the man saw us at the pier, he would bring the water to us. We were told not to be afraid of the water even though the truck looked pretty bad.

So, on the day of our date with the water man, we woke up to see that, during the night, a one hundred foot yacht had tied up next to us.

As we were untying the bow line to go get water, two women appeared from the yacht and asked if they could go with us. Surprised, we took them aboard and pulled up the stern anchor and headed for the water mountain. About an hour later we tied up to the lone pier. Sure enough, we saw the most dilapidated truck (at least thirty years old and rusty) coming toward us down the little mountain. On the back of the truck was mounted a five hundred gallon, unpainted, unmarked dirty looking tank. The driver was guiding the truck down the small mountain road. He soon came to rest on the edge of the pier. He brought us a water hose and we began filling our tanks. I tasted the water and, sure enough, it was surprisingly good.

The water was measured in meters, so we had no idea how much we took on. We just filled each tank. We couldn't understand the Greek waterman, so we showed him some U.S. dollars. He took what he wanted, smiled and drove off in his dirty little truck. Greenbacks seem to work in any country. We stopped the boat and swam for a while on the way back. One of the women said she was an Italian opera diva. I was not so sure I believed her so I asked her to sing something, and she refused.

All of the boat people we met in Greece said we had to go to Yugoslavia so we agreed to go. Yugoslavia is a couple hundred miles north of Greece, beyond Albania. At that time, Albania was a hostile, Communist country; and the police would arrest and seize vessels inside their twelve mile limit. The day before we left Corfu, we walked a mile to get ice. We found the ice house and bought about one hundred pounds in one block. We had bought a piece of netting to wrap around the ice to carry it; but this plan didn't work too well, as the ice was slippery and the webbing not strong enough to hold the weight; so we decided to walk the mile back to the boat with this heavy block of ice on our shoulders. I called cadence like I had learned in my old Navy days, left, right, left, so we wouldn't step on each other. Every couple of minutes we would have to stop and change shoulders, partially because of the weight and partially because the ice would freeze our shoulder muscles. When we arrived at the quay, we had probably melted fifteen pounds away. We took the block aboard, chipped it into smaller blocks and placed it in our coolers. In the hot sun our cooler ice would last about two days. It was our only refrigeration. Milk, eggs and other quickly spoiling foods were kept in the cooler.

Now we were ready for new adventure. After we cleared customs, we told them we were going to Yugoslavia. They always ask your next destination although they don't really care.

YUGOSLAVIA

At 1200 Fri August 15, according to the ship's log we departed the customs dock. Yes, we had to clock out, too. We had our passports stamped and documents stamped by very serious officials. Running off starboard tank I noted we were steering 000 or due north. We wanted to give Albania at least twenty miles clearance. We even rehearsed what we would do if an Albanian gun boat appeared. The decision was that we had no choice but to be escorted to a hostile port. Fortunately, we were not apprehended and we arrived on August 16 at 0800 and checked in at BAR, the first Yugoslavia port of entry. We were told we were okay by officials at BAR but that we had to officially clear customs at Dubrovnick.

Beautiful Gulf of Kotor-Yugoslavia

The entrance and the entire, thirty miles up Gulf of Kotar was breathtaking. Imagine taking a boat through the Swiss Alps. We were surrounded by 6000 foot mountains coming right out of the little gulf less than a mile wide from one side to the other. This area is ancient. We saw beautiful churches that were centuries old.

We arrived at the little town of Kotar Aug 17 at 2100. We tied up to a lovely ancient stone wall portside. We spied a nice looking restaurant about two hundred yards from us on the water. A teenage Yugoslavian boy came to greet us. We threw him a couple of dock lines and, our bad, assumed he tied the boat off. We were playing "Grateful Dead" on the speakers. This Yugoslavian kid was impressed. The three of us walked off the quay to the restaurant. We glanced back and TAIS was about to leave without us. Henry Jr ran back, barely got aboard and threw me a line! Well, we seemed to have created some excitement. The Yugoslavian kid told us all about his family. We were the first non-Yugoslavian people he had ever met. We felt like Martians or space people. Everybody stared at us. The kid told us to be sure to climb the adjacent mountain to the old walled castle.

The next morning we began our hike up the mountain. After a couple thousand feet, the path stopped and very steep steps began. I do not like heights and had just about reached my limit of altophobia and I told him this was where I would have to stop. We could see the old stone walls of the castle about a quarter mile up. Henry said he wanted to go on. He is braver than his Dad. We could also see a horizontal short bridge (a deep ravine one thousand feet) at the top with a dangerous drop underneath. I noticed many rungs or boards on the little bridge were missing. This told me some must be rotten and not safe. I told Henry as sternly as I ever had, "Do not cross that bridge. It doesn't look safe." Well, you guessed it, typical teen! He reached the top and crossed over, stepping over large areas of the bridge with only air beneath him. I held my breath till he came back down. I could see TAIS tied up to the old stone quay from my safe but high place. She was a small green figure about the size of a roach with a miniature mast. The cautious walk down was more scary than going up, but we made it.

The little old centuries old church in Kotor was not locked so we went in. I have never seen before or since so much gold and silver in one small area. Goblets, plates, platters, paintings, inlays and not even locked.

We hated to leave this Gulf of Kotor. The churches seem to be split. About half were Muslim and half Christian.

We left Kotor on August 18, at noon, and sailed up the magnificent Dalmation Coast with snowcapped mountains in view, straight up from the sea where it was lush green with huge trees not like the barren trees of Greece.

We arrived at the port of Split at 2100 hours and tied up starboard side to a low quay. Soon, a fat soldier with an automatic weapon drove up in a horizontal phone booth with wheels. We don't know how he got in and out. He looked and acted like Stan Laural in the old Laural & Hardy movies. He said under no circumstances were we to leave the boat. A guard would be watching us at all times. When he got ready to leave in his "booth," the engine wouldn't start. So he rolled down the window and asked for a push. Obviously we would have to leave our boat to do this. We pushed him off. He waved and we just looked at each other as he waved out the window and told us to go to the hotel about five hundred yards away for breakfast. We slept well and felt safe with guards people watching us at all times. The next day we were dying for a good hot breakfast. We walked to the new hotel. It was pretty on the outside, made with concrete blocks. On the inside it was very plain. The placed reeked of lime or cement mortar. The dining room was the size of a basketball court with gray walls, no pictures, a concrete floor and no carpet. Twenty picnic tables were in line and well-spaced. There were no waiters, nobody around at all. On each table was big brown wooden bowl with about twenty five hardboiled eggs in each. Accompanying the eggs were several loaves of a hard, very dark, maybe pumpernickel bread. So much for a hot breakfast. We ate several eggs each and walked out, since there was no one to pay. This was, we decided, Communism at its best.

DUBROVNIK

We sailed on up the beautiful Dalmatian coast. I cannot find the words to describe the magistry and lush green of those dense tall mountains, much like Washington or Oregon but taller mountains.

We landed in Dubrovnik and waited on board for customs and immigration. Mid-morning, armed guards and two official looking men in suits came aboard. One spoke some English. They looked over the entire boat, I guess for drugs or stowaways. Satisfied, they sat at the settee and removed their hats to visit. I offered water. No. Beer? Yes!! We had no ice, so we gave them each a hot beer. They quickly drank their beers and filled out papers with the usual official stamping going on.

One official asked if we had a coke. We did. I opened two cans of Coke. You would have thought I have given them $3,000. They were like children. One said his son, eight, had never seen or tasted a Coke. As they were leaving, I gave the man an unopened Coke to give to his son. He was delighted. We felt like we had made two new friends that day.

Later, we went into town to shop at the market. There were beautiful pears, apples and tomatoes. We picked out ten or twelve items and gave them to a little old woman. She looked ninety, wrinkled and toothless with a faded bandana on her head. The open air market was available for vendors and shoppers alike. When she weighed our purchase on old rusty mechanical scales, I saw that she pushed her finger down to make the fruit weight more.

I looked at Henry Jr. and said, "Do you see that?" He said, "Yes!" I said to her, "What are you doing?" She couldn't understand me but she knew how to get me. She started yelling. People turned at her and us and one of those scary soldiers started walking toward us. I quickly pulled a couple dollar bills out and gave them to her with a smile. She gave me a toothless grin, knowing she had won. Little scenes like that are memorable but insignificant in the grand scheme.

Dubrovnik is a little city rich in history. It was built about seven hundred years ago in the form of a walled in fort. We walked around the top of the wall which was so wide you could drive an eighteen wheeler with its trailer around the top of it. The ancient planning engineers had done an incredible job laying out the city. For example, one day it rained very hard while we were in town. The drainage was so complete on the cobble stone pavement that it was totally dry in fifteen minutes, not a puddle in sight. Much of the thick wall borders on the Adriatic Sea and it's probably eight stories above the water. Quite a sight.

While walking the wall one day, I saw an old lady hanging out colorful laundry on a clothesline thirty feet away. She looked much like the produce woman with the bandana and no teeth. I focused my camera and took pictures of her. She, too, yelled and shook her fist. This time there were no guards around. Angry people those Yugo's. That picture is probably one the best I have ever taken. Too bad the film, along with my camera, was stolen six weeks later, probably by some young punk.

We tied up Mediterranean style, anchor out and other end tied to the quay. We were fortunate to tie up next to a beautiful three year old LaFette 44. Soon the couple aboard (they were Gordon Abercrombie and Barbara) welcomed us to Dubrovnik. They asked us to come over for a visit when

TAIS was secure. Later in the afternoon we went next door. What a delightful couple they were. Both from California, they had bought the boat new and sailed it through the canal and across the Atlantic with some buddies three years before. Since then, the couple would fly over from California and spend a month on this gorgeous yacht, using Dubrovnik as a home base to sail up and down the Dalmatian coast. He was banker. She was a writer. Both were very well educated and very nice. They knew the whole Mediterranean really well and loved sharing their sea stories with us. Their local knowledge of Yugoslavia, cultural do's and don'ts, was extremely helpful. Gordon said he was envious of our journey. When they left, we missed them. They missed us too as we were a buffer for their marital squables. It's incredible how cruising brings out trust and intimacy with people that you know are going to be very short term friends.

The water in Dubrovnik was ice cold out of a spigot, again, coming out of the mountains. The mountains are huge, 6,000 feet out of the sea. When in a port we would take showers with a hose on the dock if available. The marina in Dubrovnik was such a place so we took daily showers. The only problem was anticipation of the bone chilling water and the brief and I mean brief shower itself. Wash down, cut water off, soap down the quickly rinse the soap off.

When we decided to leave Dubrovnik a 'Bora' began to blow sixty to sixty miles per hour, winds howling down from the mountains. It blew steady for three days. All the sailboats, including TAIS, were leaning about thirty degrees at the dock. After the fifth day, the bora slacked off to about thirty five knots. We decided we could venture out, since the wind and sea were at our back. We said goodbye to our friends, who hated to see us go. I believe we were a welcome relief to a crumbling marriage. It is amazing how quickly cruising people are accepted by each other. In a week, we became good friends

We learned that different countries have names for their strong winds. In France, it is a formentera, in Spain, it is a trimentana, in Yugoslavia, it is a bora. You can hear the bora roaring down the mountain in summer. It is a welcome coolness. A bora in winter must be very difficult for people living there!

Henry put up a working jib and we headed out into the Adriatic Sea, bound for the heel of the boot of Italy two hundred fifty miles south. The seas were heavy. We were riding them with just a jib. This is TAIS weather- She liked the heavy weather. We were realizing by then thatTAIS is much tougher than her green horn owners. She can take care of us as long as we do right.

Late that night, I did a really stupid thing. I got a sat nav fix and set a new course of 235 degrees except I yelled to Henry to steer 325 degrees, exactly 100 degrees too far west. It was dark and we were in the middle of the Adriatic, out of sight of land. Several hours later, Henry said he saw a flashing light off the starboard bow. We timed the flashes. It was a lighthouse or buoy. How could this be? I went down below and checked the chart. No light on our projected course. I took another fix which put us about ten miles from the Italian east coast. We didn't really want to go there, but that seemed to be the direction we were heading. When I asked Henry what he was steering, immediately I realized I had transposed two numbers, something I often did with a phone number. It is a good thing Henry was not asleep or we would have crashed TAIS on the rocks. They say that in woodworking you measure twice and cut once. Well this should also be true with navigation- double check your numbers before setting out on a course.

That same night we wondered if something else could go wrong. We were far enough south and west that the Bora stopped completely. We were in dead calm the wind that is. The sea continued to be heavy and a cross wave developed sending up fifteen foot spouts going in opposite directions. We cranked the engine but the waves rolled us badly TAIS would naturally lay side to the waves in most weather. We tried different angles with the rudder but she would not put her bow or stern to the waves. With her fifty foot mast and leaded six foot keel, TAIS was a perfect fulcrum, and we were helplessly being rolled around by the relentless waves. We would start the engine but a heavy thirty five degree roll would shut off the engine. We got out the manual with flashlights. After reading we assumed we had a vapor lock. We studied instructions on how to bleed the injectors. This is hard enough at the dock in daylight, but in a nasty crazy crisscrossing dark sea that sending up fifteen foot high spouts going in opposite directions and crashing into each other. We had a problem. We had been running off the port fuel tank, so we switched to the starboard tank. We bled the six injectors and she started, Thank God. We both were about to be seasick, standing on our heads in a stuffy engine room for hours, bracing ourselves the whole time. We learned under duress lessons not soon to be forgotten.

MESSINA TO CIVITAVECCHIA

After several hours of queasiness and frustration, of just wallowing, the wind picked up a bit and the waves started making some sense. We set a course just offshore of the heel of Italy. We seemed to create a series of ordeals for ourselves.

We rounded the heel, came right and headed for Messina. With it being a sizable city, we assumed there would be a dock and fueling station. We were also hoping to see the sword fish boats again, with their ridiculously long pulpits. Messina, it seems, was a port for ferry boats only, ferrying people and cars from Italy to Sicily and back. These boats are big, 400 feet long and five stories tall. They are ships really. They make a lot of noise with horns and whistles. We just tried to anticipate their coming and going, and stay out of their way. Right of way apparently means nothing to them. The big guy wins. We dropped sail and motored into Messina harbor. We saw no small boat or any pleasure craft. We tied up portside to the concrete cay, the surface being six foot above us. We were going to get a taxi and find some fuel. About that time, up drives an old black pickup truck with three enterprising young men in it. They spoke no English. We spoke no Italian or Sicilian. With gestures and words like petrol and diesel, gripping a garden hose nozzle, they nodded yes to everything. Off they went to get diesel fuel. About thirty minutes later, they came rambling down the quay again, this time with a fifty five gallon drum complete with garden hose and nozzle. They arrived and backed their truck up to TAIS, lying six feet beneath the dock. Henry unscrewed the fuel fill cap on the boat, and the three Sicilians leaned on the fifty five gallon barrel until it fell on its side. Now it was ready to pump. Henry began pumping, rather draining by gravity. Diesel fuel has a pungent, not-so-good, smell and I smelled nothing. I yelled for him to stop pumping. He did. I then asked him to carefully put some of the fuel in a glass. He did. No odor. I tasted it- pure water. We had just committed a seriously big mistake. Water in the fuel tank. My heart sank! I screamed at the guys. I brought the most intelligent looking one on board, showed him the engine, showed him the fuel line running to the tank. He seemed to understand. They jabbered awhile and raced off in a cloud of smoke in their old black pickup. We just looked at each other and shook our heads.

Now we had a lot work to do. Fortunately, the builders of TAIS had put a drain cock at the lowest part of each fuel tank. We got a bucket and began draining at least four gallons of pure water out. Water is heavier than fuel so it sinks to the bottom. It was a messy job, we had to drain out all the water until the diesel fuel began flowing clean.

We had just finished our clean up, when the "three stooges" arrived again, this time with two barrels. They backed up to TAIS again, pushed one barrel over. I asked to smell the fuel. I squirted a little on the dock. Yeah! It was diesel! We put the first fifty five gallons in the tank and gave them some American dollars- I don't remember how much. We didn't care at this point, and said our goodbyes.

I don't know for sure but I think those boys made some good money that day. They seemed happy as we left. As I'm telling this story, they are probably telling their children how, once upon a time, they screwed over a couple of Americans on a boat!

We cast off and motored out of Messina bound for Civitavecchia. It was afternoon when we crossed the Strait of Messina, the narrow opening that separates Italy from Sicily. We motor-sailed and sailed towards our next way point, the famous volcano Stromboli, some forty miles ahead.

A few hours later, the seas were calm, with a light breeze astern. I noticed something peculiar. The clouds were all moving from left to right except for one cloud that remained stationary. I thought, "How could this be? Could the volcano be active? And smoking? What else?" As we came closer, we began to see the outline of the volcano, then a small island to the left. I looked at the chart, which showed deep water between the two. We discussed how neat it would be to sail under a volcano and between two mountains at the same time. We could have sailed around and given Stromboli a wide berth but we would have missed the excitement of the challenge. What if the smoking volcano erupted while we were underneath? The sun dropped and a nice sunset was ahead behind the smoking Stromboli. During our year long trip we saw countless sunsets. We had begun to look forward to them, like greeting afternoon friends. It also meant that tomorrow would probably be a good day. I remembered the old saying "Sunset at night, sailors delight. Sunset in the morning, sailors take warning."

Darkness fell, but both mountains were lighted. Wouldn't you know that as if to torment us when we were between the mountains, the Tunney fisherman with their nets appeared. After our experience in Sicily, we were apprehensive. We made it through the pass watching the red and yellow glow and smoke of Stromboli. The fisherman let us through and did not entrap us as before.

This experience doesn't seem like much but how many people have been directly under or beside an active volcano in a fairly small boat? Not many. An awesome experience. Stromboli is about 1,000 feet high and one quarter mile wide. Not really very big. She smolders, smokes and send a little ash up to let people know she is still around. The inside goes to the center of the earth, which is molten. A volcano is really a valve to let off the Earth's steam so we don't have more earthquakes and other disasters. I asked Henry, now forty three, if he remembers Stromboli. He barely remembers it. We can never know what impresses a teenager.

Most people never experience this kind of adventure and excitement. I'm not sure I properly appreciated this moment either as excitement was an everyday experience according to the log. We passed Stromboli at 2300, August 25. The next morning was calm after a nice overnight sail. We were now under power. I yelled to Henry to get the glasses as there was some obstruction ahead. He said, "Dad, I think it's moving." As we approached, an enormous whale showed her huge tail. We slowed, as she was close now, swimming across our bow forty feet ahead from starboard to port. What a sight. She had to be over one hundred feet long, more than twice as long as TAIS. We finally stopped dead in the water and just marveled at this slow moving creature, waves washing across her barnacle encrusted back. She seemed not to notice us, but I knew she knew we were there. What an awesome sight! The largest creature on Earth: "Up close but not personal."

Several hours later, we motored into Civitavecchia harbor and found the customs dock. We were exhausted and slept awhile. Sleep at sea is good in intervals but something always happened to wake us up before I really felt rested, like watch changes, or there's a light ahead—something that needed our attention. We were awakened to the morning of the little old Civitavecchia seaport: noise, boats going by, whistles of ferries, the number of diesel shrimp boats and people talking, walking by. The Italians are very chatty and seem to be constantly talking. Sometimes we observed what appeared to be almost violent arguments, mostly about politics. They seem to enjoy the verbal jousting. I've noticed in my counseling practice, that when I'm working with couples, the Italian ones are comfortable with emotional give and take, whereas the partner may be reluctant to share feelings, because their cultural family of origin was more reserved or an only child. I love the passion of the Italians, and they treated us very well while we were in Italy.

We got dressed and, armed with TAIS papers and our passports, walked to customs and immigration. We checked into Italy with no problem other than the usual ritual of asking too many questions and their stamping of too many documents.

Civitavecchia is not a particularly attractive port, but very old. We had two reasons for being there. One, it was the closest port to Rome and, two we were going back home for a week.

We were told we had to move TAIS to the Club Nautico marina. We went through our routine check list of oil, bilges, gas leaks, and batteries, before cranking up. We started TAIS's fifty horsepower diesel and motored over to the Club Nautico dock and tied up to a floating dock outboard of another boat of all things! After securing all lines, we went below to clean up from our four days at sea. There was a loud rap on the cabin top and a loud voice in Italian. We went topside to meet an energetic short Italian man. He had a nice smile that was genuine. He said his name Attillo. I asked him if he was named for Attila the Hun. He was surprised that we knew of Attila. I told him that Attila was in all the American History books. I didn't dare mention the negative part of Attila. He announced with pride he was the dock master and that he was in charge. We wanted to get to know Attillo, to see if we could trust TAIS with him for ten days. He was proud of having been in the merchant navy ten years earlier and had once been in port of Norfolk. He said he liked Americans. The rule at Club Nautico marina was that boat owners had to leave a key at the front office. He had a board in his office with each boat's keys on it. We had insurance of course so we told him we would be back in two weeks. He assured us he took care of all the boats and TAIS would be safe with him. This was good enough for us; we had to trust him. This is like giving the keys to your home to a stranger.

On August 27, two days later we packed light bags, closed up TAIS, said goodbye to her and headed for downtown Civitavecchia and the train station.

Rome is inland about seventy miles from Civitavecchia. Our reason for going to Rome was threefold. One, I had exciting memories of a trip there with a wonderful wild and crazy woman I had been in love with several years before. Second, I wanted Henry to experience and appreciate the beauty of Rome.

The third reason was that Ginny had gotten tickets for us to fly back to North Carolina from Rome. My wonderful/precious/beautiful daughter was making her debut in Raleigh, the state capitol. This is an historical statewide annual event for young ladies as a "coming out" party and formal dance. It is considered to be an honor to be invited. I'm slightly prejudiced, but Virginia was the prettiest girl of a hundred plus. I was so proud of her. My friend, Carl Venters, was master of ceremonies. We stayed in North Carolina a few more days, bought a few more things for TAIS. I remember telling my brother in law Craig that Lloyds of London would only insure us on the crossing if we had three or more crewmembers. I asked him to be on the lookout for someone to crew with us, just for the crossing. He said he would be on the lookout.

The train, about a one hour ride, was fast, maybe seventy miles per hour. It stopped twice. Lots of families and kids came onboard. When we arrived in Rome, we took a taxi to the Piazza Navona.

My favorite: Bernini's Neptune at Piazza Navona, Rome.

I was hoping we get a room at a famous, small old red brick hotel covered with ivy about five stories tall. It might have had fifty rooms. I stayed there before with Althea. Henry and I lucked out! We got the last room. The Prime Minister of Italy had the penthouse. I asked the concierge if the Prime Minister was in town. He didn't know. I told him I had enjoyed a previous visit with them and had had a drink on the deck of the penthouse when the Prime Minster was out. I hoped he would he let us know if the Prime Minister was here or not so we could enjoy this treat again and Henry could see Rome from above.

We got a message from the concierge later in the afternoon saying he would escort us to the penthouse for one hour. We got a couple of beers at the little bar and followed the concierge up to the penthouse. There is a walkway outside the penthouse so we really could not see the Prime Minister's "digs," but the view was stunning. Rome, at least then, did not have skyscrapers, so we could look down on most of the city. We talked about going back in "Roman times" and what life must have been like in those days. We decided to take a bus tour the next day so Henry could see more sights and experience Rome from ground level.

I don't remember much about the tour, but Henry, who has considerable art talent, and I hope someday he will paint or sculpt some of the things we saw that day. He now uses his talent in dentistry. He loved the Sistine chapel, St Peters, and Michelangelo's David. We toured the Vatican and walked what seemed a million narrow worn marble steps to the top of the tower. From this vantage point, we could see the Seven Hills of Rome. They are still there. We could even see some of the old viaducts. The ancient Romans scored an engineering feat by directing fresh water from the mountains by gravity through these viaducts to bring fresh water to the citizens of Rome. Imagine having running water for hundreds of years using natural forces. The most stunning scene for me was in our own backyard, the Piazza Novono- three beautiful fountains sculpted by the incredible Bernini. His sculptures just seem to come alive, like Neptune could get up and walk!

PILOTING

O n the flight back to Rome from Charlotte, Henry opened more questions about navigation. I remember telling him about piloting. Math was always my worst subject in school; I could never do 'word problems' very well. In the navy as a radarman, I was forced to learn some basic math for navigation purposes. Piloting is a comprehensive part of navigation. The part of piloting that I am thinking about is coastal piloting using ranges and bearings to know where you are on the earth's surface. With a nautical chart, parallel rule, watch, compass or preferably, a binocular with a compass inside, a pair of dividers, and last, but not least, defining visual coastline points that you can see on the chart, like lighthouse, a bay with two ends, a pier, or church tower, a sailor can navigate any coast.

PILOTING PART 2

The European coast in the Mediterranean has terrific navigation points for piloting. There are so many mountains and rocky defining points. These are points of interest to see as well as for navigation points.

One of these points of interest I had never heard of but which were on some charts, were dug outs on a high Cliffside. They look about seventy feet square, with a flat floor and stairs going up to the top. These dugouts were placed strategically by the Romans 3,000 years ago as navigation points and I feel sure would be on ancient charts (if you could find one).

The person or persons manning one of these dugouts would build a huge bonfire every night so that passing ships could navigate at night. They could take bearings on these and do piloting at night. I think a large fire could be seen three or more miles at least.

PILOTING PART 3

When you leave one harbor en route to another, you need a plan, a plan you can put on paper, in this case a chart. You need a starting point, usually a sea buoy or some point close by, from which you can draw a line to your destination or waypoint. You then "walk" your parallel rule over to the nearest compass rose and line up the corresponding degree. This is your course to steer, 0 being due north, 90 degree due East, 180 due South and so on. If you stay within sight of the coast, usually within eight to ten miles, the closer the better, staying on course is easier. You take a bearing with binoculars on point A if you are going north on the Italian coast, steering 370 on your line, Point A reads 080 degrees. You then get your compass rose, lay the parallel rule on 080 and parallel "walk" it to point A on the chart (a huge rock for example) then draw a line from Point A to where it intersects with your course line. This line gives you an idea where you are since as you move further north, the angle to the rock changes. You mark the time you took this reading. To be more accurate, you can take another point, call it Point B- maybe a tower or steeple further north, quickly get a bearing on the steeple, say 005 degrees. Then you go over to the compass rose to 005 and parallel "walk" to the steeple on the chart and draw another line across your course line. Where these lines intersect is where you are. Then you write the time of your fix and draw a small circle with the intersected lines in the center. If you want to be even more accurate you can take three bearings creating a small triangle. You are in the center of the triangle.

RIVIERA

From TAIS log:

September 21. Sunday 14:45. Changed oil and filter. Engine hours 1075 Bar. 29.86. Wind north at ten knots. Depart Civitavecchia en route Portofino. Crew Henry Jr—no passengers.

September 22. 0300 steering 280 degrees bar. Rising 29.94 sailing last ten hours Island MonteCristo bears 300 degrees, ten miles off port side.

0700 calm now start engine steering 300

September 23 (Tuesday) steering 340 degrees under power 5kts, waypoint Portofino 330, 40 mi bar 29.94 sea wind calm. Low flying aircraft pass over low five to six times. Arrived Porto Rapello tied up, bow to the quay, stern anchor (Mediterranean mooring) at the yacht club. Very nice facilities."

We docked at the very quaint little town of Margeritta. Lots of sailing activity, incredible boats.We decided in Margeritta to rent a small cheap car and drive around the Riviera. Many think of France when you say Riviera, but the Riviera includes the Italian and Spanish coasts as well.

We found our tiny, and I mean tiny, cheap car and set out for Monte Carlo. The drive was stunning! Just like in *The Travelogues*, but instead of watching, you are in the show. Mountain roads, tight and narrow, one thousand feet above the Mediterranean, looking down on ritzy coves with "mega" yachts anchored. These boats are one hundred to two hundred feet long, owned by princes, kings and rich Saudis.

Monaco is tiny, but it is a sovereign state, so you have to show passports to armed guards who search your car too. We wondered if our crazy FIA captain, Dick Thompson, that was delivering the princess's boat, made his delivery, and if we might see him. He was such an engaging, entertaining person but "bad news" too! I am sure many relationships have gone south and ended as a result of his zaniness.

We drove right up to the entrance of Monte Carlo casino. We should not have been surprised, but we were. In the parking lot, Porsche's were blasé. They are pretty common in the states, but Lamborghinis, Lotus, Maserati, Rolls, Bentley's are not. They were all here, surrounding our tiny rental.

Just imagine two guys in their faded, sun bleached and wrinkled clothes, having had no haircuts or shaves in months, walking up to the big entrance casino door. On the way, I told Henry Jr. just look rich and eccentric and they won't know we are not. We don't have to take a back seat to anyone. As I expected, the tuxedoed door man let us in! I don't remember what I said to him, because we could have passed for delivery boys. Maybe he thought I was Kenny Rogers, who was popular at the time, with my gray beard and long hair.

Once inside, we breathed a sigh of relief. Neither of us are gamblers (well Henry Jr does like it some). Nobody seemed to notice us, everyone was polite because they didn't know who we were. We mostly people-watched. I expected Sean Connery, with a beautiful woman by his side, to be sitting at a table, but it did not happen. It was fun to be around the rich and famous for a while. We spent several hours watching and enjoying the place but after a while, it became boring. Cruising sailors are much more interesting. We decided, after we left, that these people were no happier than we were. It was in the wee hours when we arrived back at the marina to our comfortable old gal, TAIS.

The next day, we decided to drive to Genoa. We headed south, once again, on the scenic Riviera highway. We arrived about lunch time in downtown Genoa. We walked around, sightseeing in this old city that is so rich in history and architecture. We visited Columbus's birthplace, a tiny house in the middle of downtown. The Italians love their history. In the USA, we probably would have torn the old house down and built an office building with a plaque saying "Christopher Columbus was born here."

We asked someone on the street where we could eat lunch. We were directed to a side street and up a flight of outside metal stairs. We went in and discovered the place was packed. Just good local food kind of place the Genoans enjoy but the tourists don't know about. It was country style as we say in North Carolina. We sat at a picnic table with six to eight other people. There were at least twenty tables, with bright lights overhead, no fancy ambiance, just incredible spaghetti. We got lucky with the restaurant and we got lucky with a business man across the table, who was taking his lunch break. He was fascinated by our father/son journey. His English was better than ours and he owned a successful jewelry store nearby. He gave us his business card, so we could contact him later if we wanted or needed him.

He taught us how to eat spaghetti, twirling the fork speared spaghetti side to side not with a spoon. He said using a spoon is cheating. I watched others eating their spaghetti; no one was using a spoon.

I hate the fact that his business card was stolen from us in Marbella because he was so nice and could have been very helpful to us. After lunch he insisted we walk with him to his exclusive jewelry store. He introduced us to all of his employees and made us feel special. We laughed. He enjoyed speaking English and telling us about his family. He gave each of us some jewelry for our girlfriends which was also later stolen. I have always regretted not being able to correspond with this man. He was a most genuine, congruent man.

The Italians we met were very friendly. Most were very curious about our life on board and in the US. The next night we were wandering around Margaretta and decided to eat dinner. We were lucky again, finding a small restaurant with awnings and sidewalk tables. After a few beers, most of the patrons left. The owner, a big portly balding man, sported a huge mustache. He was a funny man and made everyone laugh. He loved people and seemed to thrive emotionally on being a restaurateur. He knew everybody that walked by. I cannot remember what we ate, but we got into a lively discussion of cheeses. He asked if we liked parmesan. We said yes. He said he had something special and disappeared. He returned with a block of parmesan, two or three pounds that had been aging twenty years! He held his arms out in a circle and said this cheese started out this big! Looking at this hunk of cheese I was reluctant to touch it. With his large butcher knife he began carving off the mold and slicing the good part underneath. This, he ground onto our main course. What a special treat. Henre Caruso was singing Aria after Aria, and our portly host was either humming or singing with him. Only in Italy can you get this immediate camaraderie and entertainment. The next day we set sail for the French Riviera and Saint Tropez.

SAINT TROPEZ

Saint Tropez is located on a small peninsula facing north on the French Riviera. A really nice old breakwater with a small opening on the west side which protects the small enclosed boat harbor. It was late afternoon when we dropped sail and motored slowly and carefully through the opening. We did not want to hit any of the multimillion dollar yachts sitting peacefully there. We noticed there was a section cordoned off for twenty, sixty foot plus racing sloops. They are called maxi racers.

We were disappointed to find no available space for TAIS. Feeling rejected, we, as instructed, motored across the little bay about a mile to Cogolin. There we tied up to an inside pier starboard side. No one was there to check us in, so we went ashore, had a nice dinner, came back and slept.

Next morning we were rudely awakened by an angry Frenchman yelling and beating on the deck house. He spoke no English. We spoke no French. He was in charge of customs and a federal official. We were in trouble in a foreign country, unable to speak their language. This customs agent thought, we found out later, we had stolen TAIS. We were flying an American flag on a boat that had Southampton on the stern. Just before calling the police to have us arrested, his assistant appeared. He was as nice as the agent was mean, and he could speak Spanish! Thankfully, he and Henry Jr. could communicate in Spanish. He checked our papers and found them ok. The agent was not happy but we paid him, so he let us stay.

We locked TAIS and walked around The Bay to Saint Tropez. There is no tide in this part of the Mediterranean so sidewalks may be a foot or two above the water, a beautiful place to stroll and look at the beautiful yachts, buildings, and people. We felt a little out of place since we were the only people wearing faded clothes. Everyone else looked like they just stepped out of an expensive store. We had long hair and beards and looked like what we were; a couple of salty sailors.

We walked up to "Drum," one of the racers. We introduced ourselves as fellow sailors cruising around. He enjoyed meeting us and invited us aboard. He told us "Drum" was owned by the drummer of Duran Duran, a popular rock band. He was a delivery crew member. They had sailed "Drum" from another port to St Tropez for a maxi race in two days. He said they had clocked her at twenty knots. "Drum" was beautiful above deck. She had flush decks, no deck house, a very tall mast, and a huge steering wheel. Below deck was Spartan, there were about ten aluminum bunks with webbing, no mattresses, and the rest of the space was occupied with sail bags. There was a very small galley. This boat was a speed machine, not outfitted/built for comfort. We felt good about being on old, comfortable TAIS. Much later, we heard "Drum" had lost her keel and capsized in an ocean race. We were happy the crew had been rescued however.

We walked to the beach and people watched. We also found a bathroom; it was made of stone, with no mortar, probably six hundred years old. It was one bi-sexual room with several twelve inch holes in the marble floor. Foot prints were carved in the floor in front of each hole to show you where to stand or squat! This was not the highlight of St. Tropez for us.

The highlight was an invitation to have a drink with the customs agent who was no longer angry. Maybe he felt guilty. He was small, clean shaven, and obnoxious. It was evening and we went to the parking lot and got into a tiny French car. The agent, his assistant, Henry Jr. and I and a one hundred pound German Shepherd dog were all crammed into this tiny car.

We went into town and sat at a curbside table where we drank too much Ouzo. Ouzo tastes like licorice. Henry Jr. and the assistant talked to each other in Spanish. The agent and I looked at each other and laughed. He told the assistant we were the first Americans he has ever liked. As we drank, we got hungry. The agent invited us to his apartment for dinner, which consisted of two scrawny chickens. The agent had a twelve year old son, who had an amazing collection of flags. Being a customs agent invites favors. He said because of his hatred for Americans he never asked for an American flag. We told him we thought we had an extra flag, which he was welcome to. Elated, he wanted to take his new friends to a nightclub so the five of us piled into the tiny French car and proceed to the nightclub.

Although I couldn't speak French, I enjoyed the music, an incredible treat. The band consisted of eight of the best Dixieland Jazz musicians I had ever heard. It was like having Preservation Hall in the same room with us. As the night went on, the packed bar got rowdier. Our host, the agent, got mean and tried to fight a couple people. Not wanting to fight or wake up in a French jail, I suggested we leave. The assistant pulled our host off of someone and we all assisted him to the car. His assistant drove us back to TAIS. Good old TAIS felt good that night.

The next morning the agent visited us. I was shocked he had no hangover. I think he must have done this frequently. We did find a small flag for his son's collection.

Our next stop was Ibiza, Spain. We estimated it would be a day and a half westward sail. We decided not to get mixed up with the maxi race, said our goodbyes and shoved off.

TAIS Log:

Oct 2: 1900 hours started engine. Departing St. Tropez St Maxima en route Ibiza steering 180.2200 Engine off sailing double reefed main, working jib sheeted to the boom- very heavy seas from the east.

Oct 3: 0320 under auto pilot steering 240 degrees 128 mile run 1ˢᵗ 24 hours next way point 233 degree 139 miles

Oct 4: 2100 sailing but barely, sea calm, wind east 7-10 waypoint 30 mi, enter harbor San Antonio Ibiza visibility low 1 mi. I was proud of our navigating and piloting 2130 stern anchor, bow to quay with commercial boats.

IBIZA AND GIBRALTAR

Ibiza is fun and wild if you like to party. The bars have live music and stay open all night, no doors or glass windows; Just wide open.

Oct 6: We started engine, upped the anchor en route to Gibraltar

Leaving the beautiful, lively, or I should say, wild island of Ibiza was difficult, but we knew we should get on to Gibraltar three hundred fifteen miles southwest. It was a glorious sail, wing and wing, with Genoa poled out to port and working jib poled out to starboard on the boom. The wind was at our back fifteen knots with a nice rolling sea.

I noticed some fish in the wave crests behind and decided to let out a feather and catch one. I had filled the reel, a 6.0 penn, with thirty pound mono and mounted it on a stanchion on our stern. We didn't wait long before the reel started screaming. I looked back and saw a big splash. I said, "Buddy we are in trouble." Whatever it was didn't slow. I fought and tried to stop him and broke the line off at the end. We couldn't stop or slow down with two sails full and poled out doing eight knots. The fish decided to go the opposite direction and the line was not strong enough to turn him. When we got to Gibraltar, I bought eighty pound test which did well thereafter. We were learning more every day.

Entering Gibraltar October 9th was easy and well-marked we tied up starboard side to the pier and had an easy check in with the customs and immigration. It was nice to have English spoken by everyone!

Soon after, I paid Nigel for TAIS. I had gone through the process of documentation. A documented vessel is much easier to get in and out of foreign countries. It is like an international approval of clear title and ownership.

GIBRALTAR

Gibraltar is mostly a big rock, kind of like Stone Mountain in Atlanta. You can see it twenty miles away. There is a city but small area wise. Gibraltar is tiny. It is however strategic. Gibraltar is England's largest navy base (I think). There is a large airport with one runway leading to the water's edge and within five hundred yards of our marina, British navy jets were a nuisance, taking off and landing at all hours. The sound is not muffled on these boys. Extremely loud. We learned to just stop talking when the decibels got up there till the plane took off.

About one hundred yards from our dock was a boathouse fully enclosed and painted dark gray. One night just before dusk a beautiful thirty foot cigarette type boat eases out into the dim light. She was dark like her house. She had six huge outboards on her transom as she squatted under the weight. She was decked over. The only protrusion was a davit or hoist for loading or unloading. This was a smugglers dream boat. Two men with black ninja outfits completed the picture. They proceeded rumbling towards the breakwater. When they reached the open Mediterranean, all six engines went full throttle and she screamed at a high pitch probably doing seventy in the direction of Morocco twelve miles away.

We believe she was at her destination in fifteen minutes. She rumbled back in through the breakwater about one half hour later, no lights showing, and into her hideaway boathouse. A James Bond like adventure. We were dying to see this boat up close and personal but we didn't dare. Henry Jr. wanted to get closer, but he was overruled.

We found what became our favorite Chinese restaurant and after dinner one night, the Henrys' rented a taxi and went to the local casino. My rule was since we didn't have much money, we allowed twenty dollars each just to get a taste of the excitement of gambling. As usual, I quickly lost my twenty dollars. Henry Jr. is smarter than me about money matters. He won I think about one hundred fifty dollars. He asked if we were going to Monaco again. I said, "No way!"

We went on a sightseeing tour of the Rock. The things I remember, other than spectacular views of the Mediterranean, were the monkeys, really Barbary Apes, guarding the rock as entrance to the Mediterranean.

They were devious little creatures. They would come up to us in small groups, begging. They had appealing expressions on their faces until we refused them. They became angry, with mean vicious faces. The attendants sold candy bars to give to the monkeys. Henry teased one, I was afraid the monkey was going to bite him. They were mean little devils, I'm sure their cholesterol was sky high from eating all those candy bars.

We were out of the water "on the hill" about a week, still sleeping aboard and using the marina facilities.

The marina of Gibraltar was a really good working marina, with welders, mechanics and tools for people wanted to do their own work too. Many marinas will not allow people to do their own repairs. This marina had a huge travel lift, which lifted our 24,000 lbs. with ease and rolled us out of the way and next to Blyss II. Blyss II was a prout, a 34 catamaran, I believe, built in France. Peter, the owner, and Lydia and two small children were living aboard and also going with us on the crossing. When I say going with us really means one hundred plus boats are to rendezvous at Gran Canary in December for the 1st transatlantic race for cruisers. Peter was from Canada. You can get a great deal on a European boat if you take delivery there, so that is what Peter did. He was an engineer and expert with ham equipment and other electronics. He set up the transatlantic networks, so boats in the race could communicate and check in once a day. This sounds comforting but we never saw anyone on the trip. All boats sailed at different speeds. I will explain later about communication at sea.

We were in Gibraltar almost three weeks, entirely too long. In hindsight, I believe we stayed so long because we were a little afraid to venture out into the big, bad Atlantic. There is safety in the Mediterranean, because land is never far away. While in Gibraltar, we blasted the bottom with the marina's high pressure hose, got all of the moss off and scraped little barnacles off. Then we sanded some of the old paint off and took barnacle plates off. We put on two coats of the best anti fouling bottom paint we could buy, Carolina Blue of course, since we both went to Carolina/UNC-Chapel Hill. We also had some welding done on the bow pulpit to repair damage resulting from a mishap in Corfu. We were bow to the quay with stern anchor. While we were in town one day the anchor dragged, I guess from some waves, and the pulpit rubbed on the concrete quay. The marina in Gibraltar did a great job of fixing it.

There was word for us that while my brother-in-law Craig was playing golf with Bruce Reinhart, Bruce asked where we were on the trip. Craig said we were looking for a crew member. Bruce said, "I have always wanted to do a crossing." I called Bruce. He said he would love to be with us. Bruce owned a Pearson 40 so he had sailing experience but he had not done much blue water sailing. He agreed to learn about celestial navigation, an area we weren't proficient in.

What is is about so many of us that we want God to take care of us, to look after us. Is it fear? Is it that we need a little help? Someone can tell us that we will be alright, but it doesn't mean much, especially when you are all grown up. But God, that's different. I am a not so good Episcopalian, not so good, meaning I don't go to church much. I am however very spiritual and getting more so as I grow old.

Since being home and having gone back to school to get a counseling degree, I have seen in my counseling practice so many miserable people, many addicts and alcoholics, many broken marriages, many ignorant kids who don't have a clue what life's all about but think they do. I have helped a lot of them but others are beyond my scope, and I'm sure my words are forgotten ten minutes after they leave my office. I have realized all I can do is try. I do think God energizes me at six or seven in the evenings when I feel brain dead. Some brilliant person said, "This is Zeus energy. That Zeus because he is king gives people special energy to help others in need."

In Gibraltar, before we left, we found a beautiful very old Gothic cathedral one Sunday. We didn't know this at the time, but it was the official British Navy church. It was filled with British naval people, from top brass to seamen in their dress whites, and their families. I leaned over to Henry Jr and whispered, "Do you feel out of place here?" He said, "Ha! They're just sailing on bigger ships!" I loved his confident response. Well, yes, we were seamen, but not shipshape. We looked the part with long hair and beards and faded clothes. We *were* clean. I don't remember the sermon, but it was about ships and the sea. I do remember the recessional hymn. I almost cried it was so appropriate.

Navy Hymn at the cathedral in Gibraltar
Eternal Father, strong to save
Whose arm hath bound. The
Restless wave, who biddist
The mighty ocean deep its
Own appointed limits keep:

O hear us when we cry to thee
For those in peril on the sea.

Previously, I had mailed my uncle, an Episcopal Bishop, a picture of TAIS to bless for the crossing. He wrote back and said he had blessed TAIS and its crew! With the bishops blessing of TAIS and this Navy cathedral service, we felt like God was with us.

I had decided when we were in Charlotte to order some mast steps. The mast on TAIS was over forty feet above the deck. We spent a couple of days installing these steps with me on deck and Henry in a Bos'n chair with an electric drill. He did a great job of hanging in this seat while drilling and screwing screws in the mast through the mast steps from the base of the mast up to about five feet from the top. This was an accomplishment for a city kid who had never done anything like this before. I was quite proud of him.

Before we left Gibraltar, we placed a large pad on the chart table where anytime we thought of what we might need to sustain three people for a month we made a list. We knew we could stop in Los Palmas, Gran Caneria but in Gibraltar was Liptons. What a great store! It was a real supermarket. We made numerous trips to Liptons. What I remember most was cheeses. The ones we liked best were the size of a softball or larger. Some were oblong but all were dipped in wax and webbing and did not need refrigerating. They were the ideal protein to store under the floorboards, the coolest place on TAIS.

The second item we bought most of was homemade bread mix. We bought about fifteen boxes. Each box would make one loaf. We tried one first, before buying fifteen and it was delicious French bread, crusty on the outside and soft inside. I'll explain later how we did this on the crossing.

MARBELLA

I had always heard what a fun place Marbella was. It was only a short drive, maybe an hour, from Gibraltar. We decided to rent a car and go. When we did we rented the cheapest and tiniest car we could find a Ford Fiesta. When you leave Gibraltar, you enter Spain and have to clear customs. We did this after working on the boat all day and locking her up. We did the usual sightseeing, wandered around the docks, looking at multimillion dollar yachts owned by kings, princes, princesses, as well as regular old Greek shipping magnets. We went back to our pretend car and put my camera bag with my Nikon, three lenses and about fifteen rolls of exposed valuable (to me) film and our passports and wallets in the trunk, the safest place for valuables. We walked from the parking deck back to the business, restaurant and bar district. I think I pulled seventy five dollars cash out. We had a good dinner and passed a bar with American music playing. It was a piano bar. A grand piano surrounded by padded back bar stools. Old American show tunes were popular everywhere we went; Oklahoma, South Pacific and anything by our favorite Frank Sinatra. We drank beer and sang along with a friendly crowd till about 1 am, when we decided to return to Gibraltar and TAIS. In those days, we didn't pay attention to drinking and driving. I've since learned better.

We reached the border, Spain on one side, Gibraltar on the other, at about 2am. I got out and opened the trunk to get our wallets and passports. All gone!! Camera. Wallets. Everything! What a bummer! The guard suggested we call the American consul. The guard dialed the number which rang and rang. Finally, a sleep voice answered. The consul was really nice, considering the hour. He said, "I can get you into Gibraltar but you can't get out." His advice was to drive to Madrid and go to the American Embassy and get a new passport. I checked my pocket, and think I had forty dollars cash left, no credit cards. I asked the guard, who said it was about three hundred miles to Madrid. We drove and drove until about four A.M., tired, sleepy and hung-over. We found a cheap flop house on the side of the road. We washed our underwear and shirts in the sink and hung them over chairs. We slept somehow on open spring four inch mattresses in a small double bed for about four hours. Later, I woke up and tried to wake Henry Jr. It was not easy to wake a teenager with four hours sleep. Not fun. Our clothes were still wet, so we hung them out the window of the car then rolled the windows up to seal the corner of the clothes. They eventually dried enough to put on by the time we got to Madrid. Henry was really good at communicating in Spanish, and he managed to get us directions to the Embassy.

The Embassy was downtown, a beautiful old brick building that covered half a block. We were introduced to the Vice Counsel, a wonderful man who addressed us and about a dozen tourists who had just been robbed. One unfortunate older couple had only been in Madrid one hour. The taxi driver had put their bag   s on the curb. While the man was paying the taxi driver, his wife turned around and said, "There goes our bags." Two boys were one hundred yards away, running into an alley.

Another woman had her pocket book/purse hooked. Two teens on motorbike rode by with a hook, like a shepherds hook. But unlike David hooking sheep, they rode close to the sidewalk, and the one on the back hooked pocketbooks like the artful dodgers that they are. The Vice

Counsel said, "These people won't hurt you, but they will steal your things." He suggested locking up in the hotel safe, all rings and valuables. After some lengthy paper work to credential us, we were free to go for a while. He wrote me a note I could give to American Express. Armed with the Vice Counsel's note we headed for American Express. A nice English speaking woman helped us. We looked pretty bad. I had a beard and long hair and Henry Jr had no beard but long hair and dirty slept-in clothes. Fortunately, she believed our story, printed me a new card and gave me five hundred dollars cash. I was as happy as I had been in a long time. We found a famous Spanish restaurant and had a beer and delicious huge paella. We then went back to the Embassy, flushed and feeling good again. We turned the Fiesta south, back to Gibralter, with our new passports and American Express card. The trip back was more fun. We stopped at Sevilla, and toured a castle. In fact, we saw seven castles along the way.

This adventure was our signal to get the hell out of Spain. We decided to leave Gibraltar the next day. We were ready anyway, but had been procrastinating.

FROM GIBRALTAR TO MADEIRA

Leaving the security of the Rock was difficult and we felt mixed emotions. After all, we had spent the last five months getting experience and getting used to TAIS, all in the Mediterranean. The Mediterranean can get rough, but there is a lot traffic. Land is never far away, so chances of rescue are very good, should something catastrophic happen. Our biggest fear in the Mediterranean was getting run over. The Atlantic is a different ballgame and we knew it.

We had spent three weeks in Gibraltar, entirely too long. It was easy to procrastinate when we felt apprehensive about the forthcoming event. I have learned that anxiety is just worrying about the future. The future for us was going through that tiny Strait of Gibraltar into the Atlantic Ocean. In that narrow strait, you can see land easily on both sides. We were warned about the strong current so it was important to catch an outgoing tide. We were told the Atlantic is slightly higher than the Mediterranean so the incoming tide is fierce, about six or seven knots. Our top speed was eight knots, wide open. The strait carries an incredible amount of traffic. Hundreds of ships are steaming into the Mediterranean; others going out into the Atlantic each day. Ships going east or into the Mediterranean stay to the right, on the Moroccan side. Ships entering the Atlantic hug the Gibraltar side. Nov 3. 1330, we departed Sheppard's Marina to catch the falling tide. We stayed about one quarter mile off the Gibraltar side, heading towards the Atlantic. All went well until darkness set in. The wind died to six knots. We were under power anyway motor sailing to get extra speed. Like it is supposed to, the tide changed. We were making very little headway; in fact, we wondered if we could be going backwards. We finally passed Terrif Point. That night was pretty hairy/scary, especially for Henry Jr. I had experienced heavy sea traffic in the navy and we were used to traffic, but not like this! Big ships don't see you and cannot react fast enough to get out of the way, so small boats have to take evasive action. Forget about right of way. We felt like a Fiat on an interstate full of eighteen wheelers. Running lights on ships are similar to boat lights, but everything is bigger. There is an all-around white light on the mast; starboard side has a green light that shines ahead to 90 degrees. The port side has a similar light on its side, but red ahead to 90 degrees. Then there is a white stern light. A ship may be eight hundred foot long, but when it's a black night it is difficult to judge its length. Also, ships at night will very often douse all the house lights underway so they can see without a glare. For example, you might see in the distance a red light and a white light but nothing else, no silhouette, nothing but these two lights. You know you are looking at a ship's port bow or down her side to 90 degrees. What you don't know is her speed, her size and how her course is relative to you.

I had a lot of experience with this in the Navy as a radar man, but we didn't have radar. What we did have was really fine binoculars that had a compass and a light inside. I had already taught Henry that a constant bearing decreasing range is a collision course. We spent much of the night taking bearings on ships' running lights and altering course. I tried to get a nap. About two hours later, Henry woke with six ships coming at us from all directions.

According to the log, we came left to 250 degrees, bound for Porto Santos, Madeira. At midnight we took a sat nav fix and changed course to

260 degrees making 6 knots still under power, with very light wind and small swells. According to TAIS log, the wind was from the NW at five knots.

The next morning, at noon, the wind picked up at our back. We put up two Genoas, poled out wing and wing, and cut off the engine making six to eight knots. At 1600, the wind shifted some and some came from the east at about twenty knots, with the auto helm steering but TAIS was wandering with a following sea.

Nov 5., the wind came around to the north. We lowered the starboard Genoa, unpolled the port genoa and set the cruising genoa and reefed the mainsail. The next day, mid-day, we were running wing and wing again with wind behind us.

TAIS has twin forestays, which are a great plus for a cruising boat. Stays are the front and aft cables that hold the mast up. Most sailboats have only one forestay. A genoa was hanked on each. When sailing this way, the two large sails work with each other as the boat rolls and wind spills from one to the other so they are constantly 'working' with each other and against each other. So we were three hundred miles from land on a small sailboat, doing seven knots, with a twenty knot wind off the stern quarter, running wing and wing with a swell off the starboard quarter making TAIS roll with each wave. Suddenly, a big storm cloud appeared out of nowhere, coming towards us. The cloud looked like it has some wind underneath. These squall clouds, if they have black wispy fingers hanging down, mean one thing to a sailor, WIND (don't know if we could be called sailors yet). Henry Jr. was down below. I yelled to him we had to reduce sail. He scampered up the ladder and up to the foredeck to drop the sails. I brought the boat into the wind with sails flailing and beating; they are very loud and they wouldn't come down. I noticed a tangle about thirty feet up the forestays. One genoa had crossed over to the other stay and attached itself.

This would not allow the sails to drop. What a dilemma! With a storm brewing, how could we fix this? We decided to rig the bosun chair and send Henry Jr. aloft. I should say, I decided because I am fifty and afraid of heights, and Henry Jr. is eighteen and not afraid of heights. A bosun chair in its simplest form is a board about fifteen inches long and eight inches wide with two holes in each end corner. Like a child's swing hanging from a tree in the country. We attached the harness on the chair to a spare halyard form the top of the mast. Henry Jr. got in the chair. I made several turns on the winch on the mast and cranked him up the mast. We had mast steps he could have climbed, but the tangle problem was fifteen feet in front of the mast on the forestays. In order to get to the forestays thirty feet up and fifteen feet out, Henry Jr. had to gather himself against the mast and propel himself out with a desperate heave. Because of the boats roll, his first shot sent him about fifteen feet out over the ocean, ditto on the other side. After numerous tries and adjusting his timing before lunging, he succeeded and grabbed the forestays. Untangling was no problem. I let him down; he hit the deck and wiped his brow as a sign of relief like, "I did it." The sails quickly dropped. The working jib replaced the genoas while the storm passed. Learning is not always easy. I guess the lesson here was to think before you act, don't panic, and have an "I can" attitude. I was especially proud of Henry Jr. that day. He learned fast.

We had about a day left before our landfall at Portos Santos. We decided not to use the sat nav the rest of the way and take a celestial sun sight at noon to get our position. My attention deficit disorder has an incredible effect on the part of my brain that does math. My whole school life in math was a disaster. Henry was not gifted in math, but was light years ahead of me. Going into huge books, looking up tables, adding subtracting, "ciphering," as Jethrow Bodine would say, was not for me. What I was good at was working the sextant with practice. It was fun to bring the sun or a star down to the horizon with some degree of accuracy. We took the noon sight at exactly 12:00 GMT and Henry Jr. went below to work the tables and do his "ciphering." He worked and reworked the numbers. I plotted his coordinates on the chart and we figured we were about one hundred miles off our dead reckoning line. It was pretty calm, so we set up the little Honda generator and plugged in the thirteen inch TV with tape deck. Before the trip in Charlotte, I had ordered William Buckley's video, "Celestial Navigation Made Easy." This title was a misnomer, and we were cussing Mr. Buckley trying to find our way. We later broke down and got a sat nav fix. If God were looking down on us, he must have thought we were the silliest two guys in his flock, and that he's better watch over them or they will never make it across the ocean.

We saw the tip of a 6,000 foot mountain on Porto Santos dead ahead thirty five miles away! Although we were certain where we were, there was always an element of doubt; so when we saw landfall, it was cause for celebration. We passed Porto Santos twenty miles and sailed to Madeira arriving at 1600 through the opening in the seawall at Funchal, the capital.

GROWING UP

Note: I think it's important for teenaged boys and girls to experience some things in their life which helps them with their sense of self so they can be healthy successful adults in life. How can we be successful if we don't know who we are? How many Jonathan Seagulls have been written about our sense of self. We have to find it to become men. Otherwise, we are lost and just drifting around in a sea of uncertainty, stuck as a teen.

This kind of outward bound experience is so wonderful. To have to rely on yourself and on another person and often just by yourself. For example, standing a wheel watch by yourself at midnight with no moon, underway. You are it, the on deck officer, what do you do when you see a red light and a white light? Dad is asleep. You are alone. It is your decision. What course of action do you take? You just know because Dad has taught you that the red light is on the starboard side of the ship. If the white light is higher, you are looking at his approaching starboard side. Since you can only see the lights and his hull, you have to guess a little. The best thing to do is take a bearing with the binoculars. If the bearing is consistent or remains the same, you are on a collision course. Maybe you should come right a few degrees and let him pass down your port side, take more bearings every five minutes. If the bearing starts widening, you know you are okay and he is passing safely. This can be very hairy/scary, especially in a busy place like the Strait of Gibraltar or a busy harbor. Henry Jr. was instructed to wake me if he felt unsure of himself. Sometimes he did wake me, and I didn't know the answer. Sometimes you just have to wait and see how things develop, then make a decision, maybe a quick one; but what a great experience! Real life experience. Survival experience. A great confidence builder. The thing about teens is they don't know or appreciate what's going on with their maturation at the time. They appreciate it later.

We dropped sail and motored through the tiny opening in the massive ancient seawall. We looked over the small harbor for a place to dock TAIS. Docking facilities at Funchal were very Spartan but typical European. I read where Christopher Columbus' first wife was from Madeira. They had a home on Porto Santos twenty miles north. The Quay must have been built in her time. There were no floating docks. We didn't see much of this in Europe. So, in order to accommodate the one hundred sixty plus boats, we had to raft up. Rafting up is when one boat, the inside one, in this case ties up side to the quay and ten or more boats tie up, side to side, to her. This requires breaking out all bumpers and fenders because the boat has to be protected on both sides, unless you are the end boat. We were in the middle. Just imagine having to walk over half dozen boats to get on or off the dock, or having people walking across your boat all hours of the day and night. One thing about boat people, they are usually friendly and happy, and almost always willing to help or give advice. They love what they are doing. They are individuals. They are different and they know they may need your help on the shore or on the sea at some time.

The quay was a ten foot walkway with a five foot seawall of concrete. This was colorfully painted by artists aboard transient boats, brave or foolish enough to be three hundred miles out in the Atlantic. Henry with his artistic touch wrote, The Henry's TAIS Nov 1986. I wonder if it is still there?

Greg Tichy was rafted to us on the starboard side. Greg had a wild story to tell. He was from the Chicago area, married with a couple of kids. He had a high paying job as an electronics engineer. Something had happened to the marriage and he had lost his job. They went to court for legal separation, and the judge ordered him to pay several thousand dollars a month. Greg was unable to find similar work and got deeper in debt. He went back to the judge to reduce his payment. The judge wouldn't budge. He thought about killing himself or going to jail. He didn't like either of those choices, so he decided to run away. He wrote a letter to his family and told them he loved them, then drove to New Orleans, sold his car and bought a twenty eight foot sloop. He named her Delta Dawn. Greg and Delta Dawn sailed over to Florida, then around the east coast of Florida to North Carolina and across the Atlantic to Gibraltar. Greg was a slight man with a thin face. He was a prototypical engineer and didn't engage in much small talk. He had been living by himself for over a year on tiny Delta Dawn. Greg was the cheapest man I ever met. He said he lived on $3,500 that year, doing odd electrical jobs on boats. He was delighted to have company in such close proximity.

Greg was a movie buff. We had a small Honda generator and a thirteen inch TV and VCR. Greg must have had one hundred movies! Several nights we would put the generator on the bow, run a cord to the cockpit and watch movies. People from other boats crowded around, sitting and standing, watching this tiny black and white TV. (This life is much like camping. If it's all you have then you enjoy it. Isn't that the way life is supposed to be anyway?) We stayed in Madeira nine days and truly loved it. Movies almost every night watching a tiny screen in the cockpit under the stars with happy people. People are funny. A number of good friends from home would not join us for a visit because we did not have running water or hot shower. One friend even said he could not be without "The Charlotte Observer" delivered daily.

If there is a Heaven on Earth, I think it would be Madeira. High on the mountain in the clouds, there's a moving fog. Like in a plane or on the ground, the clouds look solid but they are really a dense fog. Madeira is heavenly. The people have a kind sweet air. They are unbelievably friendly and clean. In fact, the whole island is litter free and clean. . They speak Portuguese, so Henry's Spanish was of little help/use. We had a camera problem one day and needed film. We stopped a man on the street in Funchal and tried to communicate with him using charades; he smiled and motioned us to follow him. We made a couple of turns and he stopped in front of the camera store, went in and introduced us.

The sidewalks in Funchal are mosaic tile, small tiles only one inch in measurement. One area had been dug up for some repair work and fresh sand surface put in. About one hundred school children with an overall scheme to see were putting the puzzle back together piece by tiny piece. They seemed to be having fun with this community project. I can just imagine this in the U.S. We never heard a horn blow. If we wanted to walk across the street, we could just go ahead. Cars with smiling drivers stopped for us. We felt as if we were on another planet.

Madeira is an absolutely gorgeous island, the most stunning of all the places we visited. It is tropical, not like the Caribbean with jungle or the rain forests, but a different kind of lushness. For example, Bird of Paradise grows and blooms wild on the roadside. Poinsettia that we have in little pots around Christmas bloom wild on trees six inches in diameter. Tropical flowers are everywhere. There is a large enclosed market as big as a football field. In this market are plants and cut flowers, hundreds and hundreds of different varieties for sale.

In this same market are scores of booths with women selling their fine lace, a trade Madeira is famous for.

We stopped in an ice cream shop. We were the only two customers. Two young attractive women were behind the counter. Both holding their hands over their mouths giggling. By this time, I not had a shave or haircut in five months. My hair was white mostly and in a ponytail. One girl asked Henry Jr. in broken English "Is that Kenny Rogers?" pointing at me. Henry looked at me. I nodded. They laughed and giggled and stared at me. We ordered our ice cream and told them we were making a movie. She handed me a pad and pen. I wrote "Best wishes for a life of happiness. Love Kenny Rogers. It made her day and mine. I doubt if Kenny would have minded. It made someone happy and me feel rich and famous for a moment.

We were told there was an exciting hike from the mountain down a goat path through the terraced farm land. One day we took a bus to the top early in the morning.

Cruising buddies told us this was a little scary, and that the railings were natural limbs cut from trees and nailed together. I worried about this, from the "git-go," but Henry Jr. wanted to do it. I've already mentioned he has no fear of heights. His "chicken" Dad, however, is different. I'm old enough to be scared. At least, that's my excuse. We went up to the mountain in a public bus, to the top; and the driver told us where to go from there. When we got to the "jumping off" point I looked around. There were no people in sight, no life savers. I got a look at the narrow goat path. Now I am one heck of a lot wider than a goat and goats are surefooted and born to climb. Henry Sr. was born to swim, not climb. I looked at those skinny makeshift limbs and decided they were just for looks and not really practical to keep someone like me from falling 100+ feet. Henry tried his best to talk me into going. I just wouldn't budge. I felt so "chicken," so wimpy. He wouldn't go without me, so we went to the famous winery where they make Madeira Port. Winston Churchill drank Madeira with his cigar every night after dinner. We sampled and sampled until we could barely walk, then stumbled back to TAIS.

We visited a very unusual garden another day. Situated on numerous acres of land. The originator years ago, maybe a botanist, had gone over the world collecting plants and flowers in tropical areas. He brought them back to Madeira and planted them. Many are prospering even though they aren't indigenous to Madeira but nevertheless beautiful.

TAIS had many wonderful qualities. One not so wonderful was the cabin sole or flooring. The original owner, to save money, had told the builder he would finish the interior himself. He never got around to it. I decided to put in a nice teak and holly sole when we got back to the states. Meanwhile, I got tired of the old dirty plywood floor and decided to paint it. We dogged (closed) the forward hatch and main hatch. We began painting forward going back towards the stern, through the main cabin, down the narrow passageway, past the engine room, finishing in the nine foot cabin and escaping out the aft hatch. We had packed an overnight bag with enough stuff for one night so we wouldn't have to breathe the fumes while the paint dried. We headed towards town on foot. Much of Funchal has cobblestone streets. We found a small Inn on the left with a miniature sign and small entrance. I figured this place must be cheap. I paid the man at the desk twelve dollars and followed him upstairs to our room. The hallway was narrow and dark. On our left was a wall, or I should say a partition about seven foot tall, missing the ceiling by two feet. Every ten feet there was a door with a number. He opened one for us and gestured this was our room. The attendant/desk man left and came back with two small towels and wash cloths. The bed was at least a double with iron frame coil springs and stuffed mattress. We started to leave, then decided there nowhere else we could stay for twelve dollars! On the dresser sat a two foot blue and white pottery bowl with a large matching pitcher full of water sitting in it (our shower). On top of the dresser with the washcloth was a small bar of black, bad smelling antiseptic soap so popular in Europe. The single window in the room was about forty inches square no frame, no glass. Two green shutters outside closed out the light. I told Henry Jr. this was a room right out of "Tom Jones." He was too young to remember "Tom Jones." If I had had a turkey drumstick and a mug of beer, I could have passed for Albert Finney. We threw the shutters open to let some air in and looked outside. There were no screens on doors or windows thank goodness. We never saw a flying bug or fly our whole stay in Funchal!

We came upon the Funchal movie theater. It was a 1930's Art Deco marquee with large letters that showed "REMO WILLIAMS" playing. We paid a couple of dollars; everything was cheap. We sat down and immediately started laughing. Remo Williams was speaking English with Portuguese subtitles! What a treat for two guys who had not been in a theater in six months. We managed to sleep that night despite the coil springs squeaking all night when one of us turned over.

The john or toilet in our room was a two step up wooden throne like a royal blue shoe shine stand. The center of the seat was a nicely cut out ten inch hole. Well-worn from six hundred years of bare butts to smooth it out. Maybe Columbus used it? I peeked in the hinged compartment underneath the hole and found a wide bucket of water with chlorine in it for the droppings. A novel experience, but it did the job. After our sponge bath next morning we argued who was going to throw open the shutters and throw the water from the bath bowl out the window onto the cobblestone street. I let Henry Jr. have the privilege. He looked both ways and let it go. Albert Finney would have been proud of us. We still laugh about this.

Admiral Halsey said: 'There are no extraordinary people…Just extraordinary circumstances that ordinary people are forced to deal with. "

We had to leave Madeira! But the weather said no. We had a two day sail in open ocean to Gran Cannerie Island, and a couple more days to get ready to race across the Atlantic Ocean. The wind has been blowing forty knots from the north for a while now.

We had TAIS ready for sea. "Mover" had just left the breakwater. The captain radioed us an hour later and said it wasn't so bad. Henry Jr. and I felt the wind slack a little. We said, "Let's go!" At 1500 we started the engine, untied the lines to the fifteen boats we were rafted to and slowly backed away from them. It was afternoon (TAIS log) when we cleared the breakwater. I brought TAIS into the strong north wind. Henry Jr. quickly raised the working jib. It instantly cracked and popped and filled with air as I turned TAIS to the south sailing under working jib alone. We were at hull speed in probably sixty seconds, steering 160 degrees towards Las Palmas. We anticipated a long two day sail.

The wind had moderated now, to about twenty five knots. The sea was very heavy, blowing for a week unencumbered by a land mass for a thousand miles. We talked about our sadness at leaving this most beautiful of places. But Madeira slowly became a small speck, only a memory.

Night came and the wind picked up to thirty knots, gusting forty knots. The waves were now mountainous. They were as high as telephone poles. Scary high. Turning back was not a choice.

We set the trusty wind vane, a mechanical self-steering device. In the dark at sea everything changes. You lose your depth perception. Also the demons come out to play. From crest to crest was about one hundred yards. The white caps, or crests, may be ten feet tall and breaking. We would surf these over and over and over. A loud hissing sound notified us that a wave was cresting and about to break. The wind blowing the foam and white water tip off the wave causes the hissing.

I was fearful of a rogue wave four times larger, pitch poling us end over end, but TAIS surfed very well. If a boat's allowed to broach, or turn side to the waves, the next one will roll you over; so steering is difficult, precise and tiring. Now I know where the term 'high seas' comes from. We were sailing under working jib and double reefed main. The working jib is well named. It really is the workhorse on most boats. It is made of a heavier sail cloth and much smaller, so it is cut higher above the spray. If the wind were strong enough, TAIS would have sailed at hull speed, under working jib alone.

In psychology sometimes I use a simple but effective exercise by William Glasser using love, power, freedom, and fun.

Glasser's Theory is if a person can create some of each every day, he will have a chance for happiness that day. I ask clients what do you do for fun? List three.What do you do for love? List three. What do you do feel freedom? List three. What do you do that gives you a sense of power? I believe men, especially have a need for power to feel whole. Guiding a 20,000 pound boat solely with your two hands and brain down the face of huge waves hour after hour is the ultimate power experience. One I will never forget nor do I want to experience those waters again. When seas have run for thousands of miles unencumbered and pushed by high winds, the waves grow and get very large and ferocious.

In psychotherapy one of the things people fear most is being small. Being small, as we all once were, can be very scary and helpless. It is the fear the inner child has, as an adult, of childhood memories.

Being on a little boat alone with a teen five hundred miles from land with telephone pole high waves descending on you, was terrifying. It's like a nightmare! No one wants to die. But the possibility of dying is scary enough.

The seas continued to build at least twenty feet. Now the seas were behind us. We decided to drop the main sail altogether, as TAIS was getting too hard to handle. This weather was our first real test of us and TAIS. She sailed much better with just a small jib (the working jib). Each sea would build up from behind to a crest then a white cap would crumble off the top. I was used to little white caps like three feet. These white caps were on huge waves and were large themselves. It would be suicide, of course, but a surfer could go overboard and ride these 'white caps.' They were breaking waves on the tips of larger breakers.

TAIS is heavy, over 20,000 pounds with a round bottom and six foot keel and these waves were tossing us around like a plastic toy in a kids bathtub.

It was a strange feeling, but as a wave would build, TAIS would seem to back up to it. We weren't going backwards. The sea was coming to us in relentless pursuit. As TAIS would present her stern to the wave, the wave would crest. We could look up and see it on top of us. But just as it would break TAIS would sail out from under it. Over and over and over a thousand times. Sailors fear a rogue wave, one much larger than the rest, breaking or pooping on you. On most of the ancient sailing ships there was a poop deck. This was a high stern deck high enough so a poop sea would not crash into the boat.

That was our fear as well as the old timers. We found ourselves thinking about how on land things change dramatically over time. Things grow and shift and erode so that much of the land on earth looks very different today than in the 1400's. On the open sea, however, the water, wind and waves look the same as they did when the ancient mariners were exploring the high seas.

When the sun went down, it became black dark. Although we had grown somewhat accustomed to the constant beating we were taking, it was different in the darkness. A whole new set of fears come on in darkness. The world changes. Another fear. We take for granted seeing where we are and what's around us. When it's black dark, we couldn't see. However, the white water always glows and the more we saw it, the less we wanted to see. Senses heighten and imagination wakes up at night because you lose sight. Hearing becomes more acute. We didn't notice it during the day, but at night a loud hissing noise would warn us of a large wave cresting on over our stern. The hissing was the wind blowing the foam crest off the top of the breaking wave. When we heard this, we felt compelled to turn around and look, over and over and over.

I once heard an interview of someone who was held captive tied to a chair. His captor every now and then would pull the trigger of a pistol to his temple. The freed captive when asked how this must have felt said it was the most frightening thing he could imagine; but after enduring this pistol thing numerous times, he thought, "Just go ahead and shoot me."

In these conditions, we were harnessed with a five foot tether with snap, hooked on a life line. We had two lifelines. One three quarter inch line was attached to the bow cleat and ran over the top of the house and attached to a stern cleat on starboard side. The second lifeline attached to the same bow cleat and ran on port side of the mast on top of house and tied off at port stern cleat. Each of these life lines ran right behind the back rest on either side of cock pit, so it was an easy grab or easy to hook onto. This was our rule in open ocean, especially at night or when one was below deck, to stay 'hooked up.' Another rule was if anyone was going out of the cockpit, like going forward to change headsails, they were always hooked up. If someone had fallen overboard, there was no way we could have been found.

The way the sea was running, if we tried to turn around, a wave could capsize the boat. In rough weather we always kept the hatch and boards closing the companion way closed in case we flipped or got pooped. TAIS was designed to right herself if turned over and upside down.

Another fear of heavy weather sailing is being pitch polled. When riding a wave or surfing like we were doing the bow could dig into the back of a wave and the following wave could lift the stern to go over length wise. We didn't fear this so much because TAIS was not digging her bow in that night.

About eight o' clock that night I fixed some split pea soup on the gas stove and brought it up on deck. This was no small task and took four times as long as usual because I had to brace myself and hold on with one hand to cook with the other, while the boat was tossing.

Not too long after the split pea soup, Henry Jr. got sick and started throwing up. This turned into sea sickness. He turned grey, then white and he was rendered useless and too weak to function. I told him to go down below and lie down on the cabin sole (floor). This is the lowest part of the boat and actually below the water line. There is the easiest motion. After he vomited everything he could, he went to sleep. If you have ever been seasick, you don't care if you live or die!

We had a self-steering device, an Aires Wind vane. It was a beautiful piece of mechanics and engineering. The vane was bolted onto the stern transom. It had a wooden rudder like paddle in the water and a paddle up above out of the water that caught the wind with various gears in between. Henry had painted TAIS in Carolina Blue on the paddle. We would set the vane on the wind which took some time, but when it was set right, she steered TAIS beautifully. There was an engineered sacrificial connection that would break if the vane was hit hard. While Henry was asleep, a huge wave bigger than the rest broke over the stern, came aboard, and damaged the vane, rendering Aries useless!

It was a total black night. I could see nothing but scary, relentless waves and the hissing white caps breaking. I was forced to hand steer with my wonderful but useless son on the floor in the cabin. I got extremely tired after five or six hours. The waves kept coming, like the pistol at my head. I didn't know if I could continue. This was alert steering, surfing down the face of monstrous waves. I felt like being in the woods and seeing a big Grizzly bear standing upright, growling ten feet behind. What is he going to do? Anything he wants. That's how I felt. I also felt like some Biblical character, maybe Jonah.

For the first time in my life, in my exhausted state, I sold my soul to God! I prayed to ask him to forgive me for taking my son on this damn trip. His mother didn't want us to do this. I was wrong to do this stupid selfish journey. I told God if he would get us out of this and at least save Henry Jr. I would devote my life to helping others or whatever he wanted me to do. Well he didn't answer me and we didn't end up in the stomach of a whale. But guess what? As dawn broke with a beautiful sunrise the sea moderated. Although still enormous, the waves were no longer breaking. I woke Henry Jr. up and he felt much better. I lowered him over the stern with a rope around his waist and a wrench in his hand. He managed to free the vane and pass the broken part up to me then I hauled him back aboard. This would have been a fifteen minute job in calm water, but it took over an hour at sea. He took the apparatus down below, while I steered, and replaced the sacrificial part. We put it back on the stern and were back in business. The Airies steering us! Thank God!

This had been the most harrowing night of my life. Sometimes I feel guilty about not doing better with my promise to God. He doesn't talk to me or give me a report card, but I feel blessed. I guess a life of counseling people is somewhat in that direction.

SALVAGE ISLAND

At noon on Tuesday, November 18, off the port bow, we saw an incredible sight. A wall of water five stories high, then another and another. We had reached our way point, the Salvage or Selvagen Islands. The waves rolling several thousand miles over open ocean were crashing onto the sheer rock or cliffs, throwing a column of water high into the air. We saw this before we saw the land.

After our near disastrous experience with El Toro off Sardinia, we didn't want to take any chances with these islands. We decided to move more to starboard and let the island pass a mile or two down our port side. These islands were well named. I can only imagine the hundreds of ships that have crashed on these rocks over the centuries, sending men and ships a mile deep to their grave.

I understand these islands are excellent for bird watching. We didn't see any birds on the big island but I've been told two people live there to man the light that signals ships.

Salvage Islands are one hundred eight five miles south of Madeira and about eighty five miles north of Gran Canerie. The rest of our sail to Gran Canerie was nice and uneventful.

GRAN CANARIES

We made landfall at 10:00 on Nov 18 in a haze. From the TAIS log "entering Puerto Delaluz Harbor Los Palmas, told by dock master to anchor stern, and put the bow to the quay. We tied up starboard side to "Calvados Sprit." What a coincidence! After talking and sailing with them for forty eight hours but had been unable to see them. It was "a great handshake meeting" like we had all survived the trip. "Calvados Spirit" was a beautiful new British yacht about the size of old TAIS. They had a crew of four lovely polite Brits on board. We became fast friends.

We spent the next week getting ready for the crossing. We had previously signed up for the first A.R.C. Atlantic Race for Cruisers. Jimmy Cornell organized this race. The last week in November and first week in December is the best and safest time of year to cross the Atlantic from west to east. Close to one hundred boats from twenty six to seventy feet, signed up for the 2,500 mile sail to Barbados. This was a gentlemen's' race for cruising yachts, for fun and safety.

Gran Canarie: Boats getting ready for the first trans-Atlantic race for cruisers.

A radio network was set up for the safety of the fleet. We called it "Rawhide" A ham frequency was assigned to the race. A few of these boats had Ham radio and others had single side band. Most marine radios are only good for less than one hundred miles. One boat, a thirty seven foot prout catamaran with our Canadian friends, was assigned as the network supervisor. We were all given daily staggered check in times. Information at check in was current coordinates, course and speed, and health of crew and local weather report.

Without examining this, you would think these boats would stick together. Not so. As some boats may go four-five-eight-ten knots, which doesn't sound like much; but the separation over 3,000 miles can be a matter of days. For example, the winner, a fast catamaran, was five days ahead of us; we were somewhere in the middle and seven days ahead of the a little twenty six foot sloop. There is no such thing as Coast Guard in the middle of the ocean, only around our coastal waters: so we were basically on our own. But Rawhide was a good connection, in theory, if not reality.

We had a captains meeting a day or two before the race. Jimmy Cornwell led some one hundred of us through this. We discussed the Rawhide network in great detail. Safety gear-health of crew-Did anyone need help getting their boat ready? We all started feeling excited now. A few people had made crossings before. They raised their hands so we could ask them questions after. I had already made a mental note of these guys.

One afternoon we were walking around downtown Los Palmas looking at the sights and checking out stores. A teenaged boy came up to us and gave us two tickets for a free drink. Why not drink a free beer? We walked down a few steps and entered a dark room through a curtain of beads. It took awhile to get used to the darkness from the bright outside sunlight. We stepped up to the bar and perched on our stools. We ordered a beer each.

The beers arrived, as if on cue, with two attractive skimpily dressed young women. Our needs were different. They wanted action; we just wanted to drink our beers. They actually seemed to relax when we told them we just wanted the beer. One was from Los Palmas the other from Korea. Henry could speak Spanish and acted as interpreter. They were fascinated with our sea stories and wanted to see the boat. We told them where the marina was. They said they would come tomorrow. We drank our beer and left, thinking we would never see them again.

We told our floating neighbors about this experience. Most of these one hundred plus boats were flying signal flags from bow to top of mast and down to the stern plus their country flag and associated pennants on the spread Hyllards. A very festive sight. The thought of racing across the Atlantic created high anxiety and excitement. This was not so competitive because these were cruising boats. It was more like a extended family cruise in the company of friends.

The next afternoon was beautiful. Crew members were washing fruit and veggies on the quay, bringing aboard drinks and food for the crossing. Some were visiting but most people were pretty busy.

From "Calvados Spirit" someone yelled over to look ashore. We did. A bright colored motorcycle had just parked and off loaded two striking young ladies! The bike drove off and the 'ladies' started their walk down the quay towards TAIS. Everybody on the quay stopped what they were doing and watched to see where they were going. I loved the curiosity of people and being a part of shock effect. Our ladies were dressed in short shorts just below the cheeks shorts, skimpy halter tops, struggling down the quay in their high heels on the uneven surface. Both had beautiful figures. We greeted them at the bow of TAIS, told them to take off their heels. We helped them aboard. All eyes were on the short shorts!

Some people on other boats gave us a standing ovation! We settled in the cockpit, popped a beer, and showed the ladies around TAIS. It wasn't long before the crew of "Calvados Spirit" and several other guys from other boats came over. More and more came out of curiosity to meet "the ladies." The little Korean beauty went below and found our string of beaded garlic cloves. She helped herself to several raw garlic cloves. She came up the ladder topside munching raw garlic. Her breath permeated the air and most of the guys left. The ladies left soon after. The crew of TAIS was the buzz of the quay. THOSE HENRYS AND THEIR LADIES OF THE NIGHT! The nickname "the Henrys" stuck with us across the Atlantic, Barbados, and numerous other islands in the Caribbean.

We estimated it would take us twenty days and nights of steady sailing if all went well from Las Palmas to Barbados. There was always the risk of getting in a storm, getting dismasted, and floating around for many days, so we wanted too much food and water. We made numerous taxi trips to Los Palmas for fresh eggs, veggies, fruits, canned meats. We topped off our two tanks with fresh water. I bought a twenty five gallon heavy plastic water container, lashed it to a corner of the cockpit and filled it up.

We were concerned that Bruce Rinehart, our third crew member, might not make it. We did get word that he had mistakenly gone to Palma in Mallorca instead of Las Palmas, Canaries. The following day, he arrived late at night, could not find us, and slept on a German boat. Nice people these cruisers. Bruce found us the next morning. We were glad to see him. All one hundred plus boats sailed out of Las Palmas Harbor the next morning.

> *From the TAIS log:*
> *1200 Las Palmas, Gran Canarie*
> *Nov 29 underway start of transatlantic race for Cruisers*
> *Under working jib and full main*
> *Wind SE @ 14 BAR 30.5*
> *Crew: Henry Jr., Bruce Reinhart, Bound for Barbados*

CROSSING

During this time at sea, there was no coast guard to call for help. We were really by ourselves on a tiny floating island. I often had to fight my subconscious fears of an accident, someone breaking a bone, an altercation with a pod of whales, a ship, a storm or getting rolled and dismasted. All these worries are real. We needed to be prepared for any of these possibilities but if I allowed constant worry I would not enjoy the voyage. So we sailed along vigilant but with a "que sera sera" attitude, making the best of one day, which leads to another. I was so appreciative of Henry Jr.'s easiness and sense of humor. There had been some apprehension about a new crewmember. However, Bruce turned out to be excellent crew member as well as an additional person to converse with and we became good friends.

Bruce enjoying the large swells, mid-Atlantic.

Some quotes from TAIS log.
1200 Departed Las Palmas Gran Canaria
November 29, 1987 Underway start of A.R.C. Transatlantic race,
sky was clear wind S.E. at 14, steering 090degrees, Baromater 30.5,
sea light. Bound for Barbados under working jib and main.
Crew: Bruce Rinehart, Henry Jr.
1515 changed course (C.C.) to 210degrees
20.51 started engine running off port tank engine
Hours 1354 sat nav fix @ 1820 showed us at 15degrees 14 West,
charging batteries 27degrees 58 North
2200 check in rawhide net
2212 stop engine, under main and cruising genoa
12/30 12:30 rawhide weather
Noon sight 27.01 North made 150 miles good 16.42 west
Dec 1 0700 bar falling, course 235degrees
Started engine for charging, wind E at 14 knots
Sea 3 ft r

13:03 noon sight lat 25.33 N lon 18.32 W
1445 no wind-started engine steering 240
1365 hours BAR 29.9
Dec 2 under power all day, 110 wind heading SW not enough to sail
toward Cape Verde Island trying to pick up north east trade winds.

We were not the fastest or slowest boat in the race. There were a few really fast boats twelve to fourteen knots but most were more like us averaging six to nine knots.

The first afternoon the wind dropped a little and we were explaining our sails to Bruce. He asked if we had ever flown the spinnaker. We said no. He said, "It's easy." So Henry went below and hauled the spinnaker up. Bruce showed us how to fly it. It wasn't that easy, but we learned. We did pick up speed under spinnaker, but then the wind picked up and became too much for the light spinnaker. Once we were riding a large wave, the spinnaker flew out to the starboard side almost amid ships nearly pulling us over. I was on the wheel and could not steer as we were careening down this wave, out of control and heeling dangerously. The rail was under water. I was afraid we would lose the mast or turn over. The wind slowed for a minute. I rounded TAIS up into the wind and we doused the spinnaker. That was scary for me especially since I had thought I knew my boat so well. Later on that night after supper, Bruce confessed he too had been scared. He said he had flown his spinnaker, but not in heavy seas. He was used to new boats, and he had some concerns about TAIS's age. After that experience with the spinnaker, he said he felt about good going on across aboard TAIS.

Large thunderheads from the east and north appeared many afternoons. They were huge and menacing, and black and dark grey, like an elephant must look to a bee in the grass. There is nowhere to avoid them, just open sea. As the storm clouds approached there was discussion as to whether it would be a local squall and produce heavy winds and maybe rain. We didn't mind the rain. That was welcome but squally winds can reach fifty to sixty knots in a matter of a couple of minutes. Many blue water sailors have been knocked down (turned over) by these sudden winds. What always entered our discussion and this may have been the most exciting part of a lazy day, was how much wind is the storm cloud bringing as it was coming upon us. One telltale sign are wisps or black fingers streaming down under the cloud, which meant wind or possibly a tornado, or at sea, a waterspout.

At night these clouds continued to come and go, sometimes getting very still, causing total darkness. To stay safe we would drop sails so we didn't have a fifty knots wind hit us. When it passed we would put sails back up. Rather than wallow in a trough we would crank up the engine to maintain fair steerage until the storm passed. If the wind was heavy we might put up the small storm jib. It was amazing how the tiny sail could move a 20,000 pound boat through the water at six to eight knots.

One thing about sailing, is it is basically a lazy way to get somewhere. However, when the wind picked up and lines started bull whipping, popping and sail cracking like fire crackers, all hell would break loose and we would really have to act in a hurry or something could get broken or someone might get hurt. My biggest fear was someone getting hurt. My old Navy training taught me that the more you rehearse, the more prepared you are when the event actually happens; so we would practice every day.

On our crossing, when the weather was nice we would enjoy twenty knot northeast trade wind with about eight to ten knots across the deck, enough to keep from sweating if just sitting around. The rocking and rolling of the boat, the sound of the waves slapping the hull, some occasional spray lulled us to a half awake, half asleep but always aware, state. We were like firemen, sitting around or doing busy work, until the alarm rings, and the adrenaline starts flowing and then you get in another gear, you mind clears and you do what we have rehearsed.

The waves were not directly behind us. Sometimes there would be a very, very large swell behind us, from crest to crest about the length and height of goal posts on a football field. When we were in the middle or fifty yard line, and the wind dropped a bit because you are in a hole, then slowly we would pick up a knot as we began slowly down the hill again. Within this super big base wave there would be a smaller six to eight foot wave that came across the starboard stern quarter. As we slid down that wave, while riding the much longer and larger wave, a rocking motion is created. We sailed for weeks going uphill, downhill, and rocking back and forth as we sailed. Initially this motion is not very comfortable but we adapted and our bodies got used to the cadence. Sleeping with this constant rolling of the boat can be challenging. We learned to sleep "spread eagle" so that we wouldn't roll from one side of the berth to the other all night.

TAIS had a nice walkway about two and a half feet on either side of the house or cabin. Most boats today have roller furling headsails. We didn't. In addition to the main sail we had six headsails. We had a storm jib, made of a very small heavy cloth, and cut high so waves could not reach it. Next was the working jib, which was a little bit lighter cloth and larger. This was the work horse. We could drop the main or double or triple reef the main, and the cruising jib would take us along in twenty five knot winds. We had a cruising genoa which came about halfway from the bow to mid ship. Another sail, much lighter (the one we blew out in Sicily) extended beyond mid ships. The headsail because it was light, filled easily to about fifteen knots. In addition to these, we had a spinnaker as well as a cruising genoa cruising spinnaker some called a blooper; it was very light made from parachute like material.

These sails, except whichever one was hanked on the forestay, were stored in sail bags, light canvas or dacron bags. They look like a bean bag chair with a draw string to keep the sail inside. The walkways amid ships usually had three or four of these bags between the life lines and the deck house. These bags made wonderful bean bag chairs. We would sit on one, wiggle our butts and get really comfortable. Sitting in one of these on a pretty day sliding down waves three feet from you, with a good book was a bit of heaven I shall never forget. A nylon netting attached at the lifeline and deck kept the bags from falling overboard.

Bruce and Henry loved these bags too. Bruce would listen to Frank Vest taped sermons. Henry read or wrote Suzanne. Bruce was a pleasure to have aboard, although he got a little homesick for Mary, his wife. He helped Henry Jr. with celestial navigation. I would take a sight with the sextant, and Henry and Bruce would go below and do the math tables. Sometime we got a good noon sight, sometimes we would be one hundred miles off. One thing that was reliable was Polaris (North Star). We could see it and the horizon at twilight and day break. Polaris remains steady in the northern hemisphere so if you're on thirty eight latitude, Polaris will be close to thirty three degrees north. If you know your speed, you're okay. This is how Columbus sailed across the sea. When we took a sight and the guys went below to do the math, they usually came up with an accurate fix when they plotted it on the chart.

Normally the Satellite Navigation System (Sat Nav) would communicate with the satellites in outer space and send down a "fix" which gave you your current latitude and longitude. We would plot these fixes on the nautical chart and track our course. With today's technology, you could get constant real-time updates from satellites, but back then we didn't have smart phones with GPS and the fixes only came about every forty five minutes. One day the Sat Nav went out and we stopped receiving fixes.

We tried everything but could not get the Sat Nav back up. It stayed off for about seven days so we had to rely on celestial navigation as the ancient mariners did back in the days of Christopher Columbus. Weather permitting, we would try to get a sextant sight of Polaris (the north star) and a noon sight of the sun. A sextant is an instrument that measures the angle of the sun or a star in relation to the horizon. By measuring this angle and knowing the exact time of the sighting, you could go into the declination tables and calculate your longitude. With heavy seas, this angle can be very difficult to measure. Also, if there was a lot of cloud cover, you couldn't see the sun and stars to measure. The challenging part of a Polaris sight also is that you have to time it such that it is dark enough to still see the star but light enough to see the horizon, very tricky.

Two days out of Barbados, a freighter passed down our portside. I called him on the radio. He answered and gave us a sat nav fix. We were about thirty miles off our course. Not too bad after sailing sixteen days and 2,400 miles.

Shipboard routine was pretty simple. All hands had to stand night watches. It would only take ten to fifteen minutes for a tanker coming in the opposite direction from the horizon to be on top of us. We were all mindful of this fact. Commercial ships cannot maneuver, so it is the small boat's responsibility to get out of their way. At night we went to sleep at dark and woke up with the sun. We staggered the night watches so one person was on watch at all times. In fact, we had a fifteen minute timer that we could set as a reminder. I rigged up a small bulb light to the cockpit so the person on watch could read and stay awake.

One night I was on watch. It was pitch black in the cockpit, the ocean four feet away and three miles deep. Everyone else was asleep. No one knows what's down there. I was reading a scary book when a loud slap and whoosh and sucking sound 4 feet from me occurred. I knew it was not a dolphin. It was too loud and heavy. Whatever it was, was very big. Fear set in, all alone in a small boat in the middle of the ocean. I thought about Columbus's crew seeing sea monsters. Could it be true? Probably a curious whale. I'll never know but it was frightening, nonetheless. The feeling of that fight or flight syndrome is spontaneous!

The fishing experience from my misspent youth proved invaluable. Almost every afternoon one of us would let out one hundred feet of line behind the boat, with a green and yellow feather and a hook. Within one half hour we would reel in a five to seven pound mahi-mahi. We had a flat board and filet knife handy. Within minutes the fish was skinned, fileted and carried to the galley. Depending on the conditions, I would cook the fish in the pressure cooker. I'd use salt, pepper, chopped onion, and canned tomatoes along with chopped potatoes, making a sort of stew that was delicious. Sometime I would sauté, sometimes poach, the fish in the frying pan. We never ran out of cheese. They were so delicious, which was a great delight.

Knowing we would want bread on our crossing, I had bought a package at Liptons to make one loaf. It was excellent, so we returned to Liptons and fifteen more boxes. Each morning we would run the engine for about forty five minutes. The batteries needed charging from powering the night's running lights. Diesel engines run cool, but when they are turned off, they get hot. This was usually part of our daily morning routine. The engine room would heat to about one hundred degrees. I would mix my bread put it in a stainless bowl and place it on top of the engine block for forty minutes. It would double in size. Then I put the dough in a bread pan and baked it in the bottle gas oven. It was excellent. I fed the crew well!

One afternoon the reel screamed faster than usual. We all looked astern to see a seven foot white marlin tail walking behind us. We reeled him in all three of us. It took about forty five minutes because we didn't have a rod, only a reel mounted to a stern-rail. One person would reel the line in and we would pull the line hand over hand with gloves on. Henry put on gloves reached down grabbed his long bill. Bruce took a picture, then we let the fish go. We never knew what was going to come up to the bait.

Every morning flying fish would adorn the decks, some flying high enough to sail into the cockpit. I never knew they were edible till we got to Barbados where they are fried by street vendors in large kettles- a very popular dish there.

The simple SunShower proved invaluable on the crossing. This shower cost less than fifty dollars and consisted of a two gallon heavy plastic bag with a fill hole and bridle at the top. At the bottom, a two foot piece of hose with showerhead was attached. The SunShower was filled with a gallon of freshwater and suspended from the boom or spare halyard. Our every other day shower went something like this: strip down naked, sit on the cabin top, another person dips a gallon of salt water from the ocean and douses the bather with salt water. Next, the bather soaps down, head to toes, with salt water soap and another bucket or two to wash the soap off. Finally, the fresh water (sometimes only two quarts worth) from the SunShower was sprayed on the bather to wash the salt water off. This worked quite well and was the highlight of the day. Something so simple can be entertaining when you are so relaxed with nothing else to do. Plus, the constant rocking and rolling and quietness keeps one in a slow, moving, meditative state.

BARBADOS

A couple of days from Barbados the sat nav came alive! Bruce had moved a sack of potatoes from a shelf where the antenna was. We didn't know this, but the sack had prevented the antenna from picking up the signal. Thanks to the one ship and our renewed sat nav, we were able to make land fall, Barbados! We opened a bottle of hot champagne we were saving. We hugged each other and celebrated our 'crossing' nineteen days.

Celebrate landfall Barbados! Hot champagne after eighteen days at sea.

We rounded the southern tip of Barbados and headed up the coast to Bridgeport, a small seaport with good commercial mooring and piers for cruise ships. We motored into the small boat harbor and tied up at the 'check in' dock, downtown. We were greeted with a big rum punch packed with ice and a steel drum band! The ice was as refreshing as the rum had been. We had been sailing without ice for almost three weeks. Ice is one of those simple things you take for granted. When you are at sea for any length of time, your inner ear and body get used to the motion which is called "sea legs". Some people have a hard time with this motion and stay sea sick. Henry remembers when we first stepped off the boat after being at sea for nineteen days straight, how wobbly it felt for a while on land while our inner ears became adjusted again.

The race was not very competitive for most of us. We finished about in the middle, which was good for us. I believe the winner arrived in thirteen days. The last boat a twenty six foot sloop took twenty five days. We were seconds behind a much faster French boat. Behind us we could see a Freedom 40 and a CT 43, both new and considered faster boats.

We stayed in Barbados about a month, much too long. Barbados is flat and not a very pretty island. It does have pretty beaches and resort hotels. We only spent a couple of days in Bridgetown. Our fellow yachtsmen were either there or coming in one by one. There were always cheers, rum punch, and celebration. Mount Cay Rum sponsored the race, so free rum was everywhere. Mount Cay gave us a banquet and dance one night. It was a really fun time, with these several hundred sailors. We had all accomplished something and wanted to celebrate. Henry's girlfriend Suzanne, my girlfriend Beverly and my daughter Virginia came and stayed a week. They helped us celebrate.

Suzanne washing clothes on dock-Barbados.

All of the anchorages are of course on the west or Leeward coast. Our favorite was about an eighth of a mile offshore of the "Boathouse," an open beer shack with burgers and plenty of partiers. Great camaraderie.

Our orange dingy was old and the rubber rotten. Frank Sinatra once played a part of Dirty Dingus McGee. So our dingy became "Dingus." We were constantly patching holes. We anchored just offshore of the Barbados Yacht Club for a big dance that night. Even though the Lee side is calmer, there is a swell. The swell breaks on shore like in the ocean on a calm day. Now picture Suzanne, Bev, Virginia, Henry and me all inside Dingus pushed by a four horsepower motor. When we got to the beach, we had to ride a breaking five foot wave. The girls had their best clothes on now, with wet butts. The dance was fun. On the way back to TAIS, Beverly and Virginia had to stick their fingers in holes to keep us from sinking. Henry Jr. was bailing all the while.

The Henry's, Cranes Beach, Barbados

Henry Jr., Cranes Beach

Nice catch!

We had to get rid of Dingus. After our guests left, Henry and I departed for Grenada. We had both been itching to get back to sea again. Henry by now is proficient at celestial navigation and is excellent on the fore deck. Grenada is one hundred sixty miles south west of Barbados. We talked about how nervous we were in Spain when we departed on our first three hundred mile open sea voyage and how much more confidence we had now. The trip to Grenada was an easy overnight.

GRENADA
VENEZUELA- LOS TESTIGOS

Cruising people love to talk about where they've been, where they are going next and sea stories in general. While visiting with Conrad and Jill aboard "Coquita" we discussed going to Venezuela southwest one hundred miles from Granada. Our route was to take us to the Testegos islands then up the coast to Isla Margerita. Conrad had no charts and neither did we, covering this area. We dingyed around different boats at anchor in Granada and finally found one boat with cruising charts of Venezuela. The captain said to bring tracing paper and we could use his chart table to trace his charts. We bought tracing paper only available in 8.5 x11 size. We scotch taped a number of these together the size of the original chart. After many hours of minute detail tracing, we had ourselves a chart suitable for basic navigation.

Henry Jr., wet trip tacking windward from Venezuela to Granada

Rainbow, ten ft in front of us, Granada

TAIS log states we raised anchor on Feb 5.1900 speed 5.5 knots under cruising genoa only, rolly polly wind NE in company with "Coquita" and "Serenity." We set a course of 245 degrees ninety miles to Los Testegos Islands. Testegos is a little obscene descriptive word. A larger island with two smaller ones side by side. The overnight sail was uneventful. We led the way of three boats since we had the only chart, the rudimentary traced chart, showed a channel between the two testicals with about twenty feet of water, plenty of water since we only needed six feet. What I didn't consider was waves. It is easy to get used to a swell behind you till it is barely noticeable. The space between the tiny islands was only about one hundred fifty feet. As we committed ourselves to enter the pass I noticed the swells getting bigger and bigger. The bottom was getting shallower and shallower. By the time we entered the pass, fifteen foot seas were rolling through the one hundred foot opening. Thank goodness they were not breaking but very steep as the bottom rose to meet them. TAIS did a beautiful job of staying straight and not broaching. It was a 'wipe your forehead' surfing excitement. The other two boats with experienced blue water sailors came through safely too.

We all anchored just behind the northern most Gran Testico island which is very calm on the Lee side. We put an anchor on the beach and a stern anchor out to keep us off the beach.

Conrad ("Coquito") pumped up his dingy, put his forty horsepower outboard on and came over to TAIS. We locked up TAIS, thinking she would be fine. Off we went one and a half miles across the bay to the larger island. This island has the only inhabitant on Los Testigos. He is also counsel and has proper papers to check in to Venezuela. His office/house was perched on a small mountain with some three hundred steps to the bottom and small pier. A lonely occupation. He was excited to see someone. He spoke perfect English and told us he been a Venezuela counsel based in Charleston, S.C. He loved the U.S.

We pulled ourselves away from the counsel and proceeded down the dangerous steps to Coquito's dingy. Conrad liked to go fast so we flew across the bay to our three boats, holding onto the soft sides of Little Coquita.

We remained bow to the beach for another day mesmerized by the Frigate birds. These sea birds are supreme soarers. They are large, with eight foot wing span. You rarely see one flap its wings. They circle and circle higher and higher until they are a tiny speck. They have a long split tail that helps them steer. They reminded us of Batman's spotlight image in the sky. It was incredibly relaxing to lie on a sail bag and watch as hundreds soared around.

Los Testegoes, being uninhabited was a breeding area for these birds. One day the Henry's decided to venture inland. We had been warned of wild boars. Maybe 200 yards inland we began hearing twigs breaking then grunts and squeals. I motioned to Henry to head back to the boat. Birkenstocks and wild boars don't go together.

We reached TAIS to find we had company. Thirty feet from us, a thirty eight foot wooden fishing boat was beached. It was white and covered to protect the fishermen from the hot sun. Six natives, each wielding a machete, were hacking away in chin deep water, at a mammoth manta ray they had caught. This fish must have weighed over 1000 lbs. It was eight feet in diameter and twelve inches thick. They seemed to know what they were doing. Each hunk of manta ray was about twenty pounds. We decided six natives with machetes were too close for comfort. We pulled anchor, waved a friendly goodbye and found another place to spend the night.

Next morning we ate breakfast pulled up the anchor 0820 underway Margarita steering 245 degrees 6 knots wind northeast 25-30 under working jib.

Feb 9 1400 landfall Margarita, Venezuela.

1630 enter harbor Papatas

1700 drop anchor 120 ft. chain in 12 feet of clear water.

A number of our cruising buddies were anchored in the vicinity. We sleep better when friends are around.

Next day we take on sixty gallons of clean fresh water and one hundred twenty gallons of diesel fuel. Fuel was an amazing ten cents a gallon in this oil rich country. Polar beer was incredible too, at twelve cents a can. We bought enough beer to last the entire trip.

We ventured inland to a little scary town about eight miles away and twenty cent taxi ride. There were no police, but armed green beret soldiers were on many corners and walking about. We had Argentine beef steak, baked potato, and salad, all for only five dollars.

One day we needed a few parts for the outboard. We found a sporting goods store, and got our parts. Outside was a used but beautiful orange zodiac dingy. I inquired about the price. The man wanted five hundred U.S. dollars. He would not reduce his price and we didn't have five hundred, although the dingy was worth more than that. With Venezuela being a police state I thought it might be difficult to buy a gun so I told him we had a gun. That got his attention! His eyebrows rose. He smiled.

The man drove us to the landing where TAIS was at anchor. The new dingy was in the back of his pickup. It held air! Henry Jr. and I pumped up old dingus and motored out to TAIS. We got the shotgun, broke it in two pieces and wrapped it in a large cloth. We dingyed back to shore, gun in hand, opened the pickup door and sat down. The nervous man looked both ways. Convinced no one saw us, he unwrapped the shotgun. He smiled a big smile. I knew we had a deal. We slid the dingy off the back of the truck, then picked up Dingus and put him in the truck and said goodbye. No more patching. This had become an everyday occurrence. Dingus was just rotten. We discussed that night that we could be in big trouble if the shotgun were ever traced back to us. We decided to go back to Granada the next day.

TAIS log: Feb 18 0900 up anchor underway bound for Granada course 130 degrees under full main and cruising genoa wind east at 15 knots 1200 wind increase to 30 knots

We were going into the waves. Our sail sheeted in tight to windward with big choppy seas spraying salt water over the entire boat. We made Granada in one tack.

Granada is absolutely beautiful! We arrived at Prickly Bay in the morning.

Prickly Bay is really a big cove protected by coral reefs and hills, rocky cliffs.

It has a small marina and bar restaurant and not much else but a palm lined beach, and clear water. We saw fifteen boats anchored. We knew six of them from Barbados and the crossing. A postcard anchorage!

One day while we were resting in the small lagoon near the yacht club, it started raining. We put up the awning draped over the boon to stay dry. After the rain, the weather was steamy from the humidity. Then a four hundred foot incredibly vivid rainbow appeared, not off in the distance but right over our bow! It almost touched our mast! What a sight! I have never been in a rainbow before or since.

There is camaraderie among most cruising people quite unlike anything I had ever experienced before. These people are from many different countries. Because of the language barrier, most of our good friends were English. We would trade small favors, such as charts, cruising info, when and where to get this or that. Anytime there was a BBQ on the beach, everyone was invited. Nobody cared what anybody did for a living and rarely asked. Everything was focused on the here and now, and where were you going next. The million dollar yachts were anchored alongside the $20,000 twenty six foot single hander and everybody seemed pretty happy. I was surprised to see so many families cruising.

BarBQue, Granada, Conrad Flowers

As soon as we anchored and cleared customs and immigration at Prickly Bay, Peter from "Blyss II," a thirty foot catamaran and net controller of "Rawhide," paddled over to invite us on a tour of the island. This we did with Peter, Lydia, two beautifully behaved small children and Peter's parents from Canada. All of us in a mini bus with a native driver. Granada reminded me much of Madeira, very, very lush and green everywhere. It's called the spice island. Huge nutmeg trees, bananas, oranges, limes, kiwi, almonds, and bougainvillea all grow wild. There is a 3,000 foot mountain with reinforcement in between gigantic bamboo clusters. We stopped at a waterfall, but were unable to catch the water. A native came walking by, stopped, picked a leaf the size of two hands from a vine and fashioned a bowl. He filled this with water, took a drink and went on. He showed us how to make this leaf container. I began picking leaves and within minutes we were all enjoying the primitive experience of drinking from a leaf bowl. It was delicious.

Silly me with worn out swim suit.

About two days later, we sailed around the south west tip of Granada to St. Georges. This is a world famous, small but deep water harbor. Cruise ships came in every day, a careenage with bright colored native schooners that come in and trade from other islands. The pace here is very, very slow. St. Georges looks a little like a Mediterranean sea village with a very low quay and at a distance. The little buildings look like they are in the water. We anchored about a half mile away, just under the Granada Yacht Club. One circumnavigator said of all the places in the world he had been, watching the sunset from the porch of the Granada Yacht club was the prettiest. Henry and I enjoyed a shower there in the afternoons, then had a beer at sunset, watching the one hundred or so Egrets swoop in and gracefully land in a tree twenty feet away for their nightly roost. They would quarrel with each other over who got which perch, but at dark, they become very quiet. The red bougainvillea became very bright, as if lighted, in the afternoon sun light a beautiful sight! The red sun was setting directly behind the harbor entrance and plopped into the sea.

Ginny came for a weeklong visit. She was thrilled to see us after the Atlantic crossing. She told us how relieved and excited she had felt when she got the call from Henry that we had landed safely in Barbados. Her friend and cleaning woman (Maurice) had called her out of a therapy session with a client to answer the call and when she heard Henry's voice, she said she burst out with tears, know that after weeks of hearing nothing, we were safe. She could not stop crying which let her know just how anxious and worried she had been the last few weeks we had spent at sea.

When Ginny arrived, she also brought along a really good book she was reading: "The Prince of Tides." She read to us at night. During the day, we sailed to several beautiful beaches and swam or dingied to shore. Once, we went supply shopping ashore. Ginny got a chance to see what shopping in a third world country was like. The selection isn't that great unless you want a live chicken or goat.

She was also surprised to hear there were still tales of pirates. You can always find things to worry about. We never saw any pirates but we were careful to anchor around friendly boats. There were a few cruise ships tied up downtown. The tourists would flood the little village and fill up the restaurants but we preferred our own cooking.

"Miller Time," a sixty foot long liner, was escorted into the downtown dock one evening. She was caught fishing too close to Granada. Her catch of several thousand pounds of fish was confiscated and her crew wasn't allowed off the boat. We spoke to the captain/owner Miller several times and he was actually a really nice man. We bought them cigarettes and drinks for the crew. In the end, they were fined and went on their way.

Virginia and Henry sailing.

ST. LUCIA
FOR VIRGINIA'S DEBUT

When we were in Raleigh for Virginia's debut, I stayed with my good friend and first cousin Jim Wright. Jim and Beverly were kind enough to let me stay with them when I was in the Raleigh area. This time we had left TAIS in Italy and flew to the states for Virginia's debut.

Jim and Beverly, Molly about seventeen and Jimbo sixteen, all wanted to hear about our trip. They wanted to come visit for a week somewhere in the islands. We had a loose itinerary and told them we would give them a couple weeks' notice. The week they chose on the phone we were scheduled to be in St. Lucia. We arrived a day or so before them and anchored.

The log states on Feb 26 at 0300 we departed the little island of Bequia en route St. Lucia steering 350 degrees, one reef in the main and small genoa. 20 knt ENE port tack. Large seas fortunately were not on our nose. TAIS is so comfortable and sturdy and secure. The Henry's are pretty salty sailors now, but never over-confident. I have great respect for the sea. It is an ego trip, however, to be able to master the wind and sea. I don't believe many people ever experienced the mastery of something so much bigger than themselves. Jumping out of a plane (which I am too chicken to do) is only thrilling for a few seconds. You can climb a mountain in a day. But day after day of changing sails, looking out for ships and whales and sunken debris, constantly keeping our balance while the boat is being

145

thrown about like a cork by angry waves. That is truly being alive. At 1600 we arrived in Marigot Bay St. Lucia. We anchored in twenty feet of water and pumped up new "Dingus" and dingied over to the customs house and checked in.

After checking in customs, Jim, Beverly and Jimbo arrived. We always looked forward to guests. As much as The Henry's love each other, it was good to communicate with others, especially family. We dingied them back from customs to TAIS, riding on her anchor and six fathoms of heavy chain. One great thing about anchoring with chains is that unlike anchoring nylon line which is light, allowing the boat to 'sail' around the anchorage, with chain and thirty five pound CQR anchor, the chain drops straight down and lies on the bottom for twenty feet or so to the anchor. It takes a pretty good wind to push TAIS life chain off and security provided by the chain far outweighs the added weight of storing it.

We got a nice surprise that afternoon as the little twenty six foot "Delta Dawn" sailed into the tiny harbor. I have written before about Greg Teechy, the lone sailor. We welcomed Greg with whoops and hollers. He anchored fifty feet from us. He came aboard TAIS and told us about his lone crossing. He had sailed directly from Madeira to St Lucia using only a makeshift radio direction finder. He said he knew if he sailed west he would hit some land. He homed in on an AM station, which was St. Lucia, from 100 miles at sea. Jim Wright was mesmerized with Greg and could not believe his story of crossing oceans in his tiny boat and living on $3,000.

Feb 27 (log) 0900 Haul anchor and sailed up the coast about 9 miles to Castries. We tied up at the small boat harbor and took on good fresh water and diesel fuel.

Tied up adjacent to us was "Wynthe," belonging to 'the most trusted man in America," Walter Cronkite Jr. She was a beautiful forty eight foot ketch built in Wilmington. I asked his captain if he was aboard. Soon Walter emerged from the cabin with his captain cap on. I introduced myself and Henry. I told him about cruising the Mediterranean and the crossing. He was a great listener and put me totally at ease. He was especially interested in Yugoslavia and said he had never been there. This seemed unreal telling Walter Cronkite something about geography he didn't know. After twenty five minutes, a tall white haired man appeared from below. I recognized him as the man who did the weekly adventure, Wild Kingdom. His wife and Mrs. Cronkite appeared and said lunch was ready and could we join them. Very polite, but we declined. We were both impressed how relaxed and genuine this great man was and how he gave half an hour of his time to a father/son duo and making it a day to remember for us.

Log: 12:00 noon underway Rodney Bay. Arrive 1400 drop anchor in 8 feet of water. This is a tricky but beautiful anchorage. White sandy palm laden beaches slowly rising upward to two tall pitons about ¼ mile inland. We were told how to go about this anchorage. We were warned about the little boats with natives. You have to pick one, and the others will go away. The man we picked was Johnson Prosper. We became great friends with Johnson, especially Beverly. Johnson took a long line from the bow and tied it to a palm tree. We dropped the stern anchor to keep us off the beach.

Johnson Prosper, our self-appointed guide in St. Lucia.

St Lucia has two spectacular cones, Gran Piton and Petti Piton. They rise from the sea below Soufriere, a little west Indian town with brightly painted buildings. Gran Piton is about 2,000 feet high. Johnson said he would take Jimbo and Henry up Gran Piton for twenty dollars. Now Johnson in addition to being a good businessman is a superb athlete. He is about five foot ten, one hundred eighty pounds, always barefoot and wearing only swim trunks and a tee shirt. We paid him and off they went in Johnson's boat. We saw their progress from TAIS as they ascended Gran Piton. Through the glass they looked like miniature climbers. Those of us on board were concerned for their safety but Johnson was not afraid of anything. Several hours later they returned, still exhilarated from a terrifying mountain climb. Johnson had to reach down and pull both boys up numerous times. Henry and Jimbo both agreed that they probably should have had some harnesses and climbing rope for some of the vertical rock walls they went up. Once on top of the Piton, they said that Tais looked ant-size in the harbor! They were two excited teenagers, proud and happy to be back aboard TAIS.

Henry Jr. and Jimbo climb the scary pitons, St. Lucia.

We decided to sail south to Beque. We pulled up anchor and set sail. When we left the cover of St. Lucia, we were in open ocean and it became a little rough. Beverly began getting sick, so Jim suggested we turn back. We did. On the way back we put out our trusty feather. Pretty soon a twenty pound tuna hooked himself. Jim cleaned the tuna. Beverly felt better. We anchored underneath St. Lucia and had a great charcoaled tuna steak dinner.

The next night we were invited to an island "jump up" in town. Thousands of people (natives) dressed in costumes for a big parade. I looked up and there was Beverly marching in the parade with a three year old native boy on her shoulders. It was a great party. People were very friendly.

We were sad to see our guests leave, but we had to move north.

GUADALUPE

March 12 10:00 underway Fort de France, Martinique 1500 drop
anchor downtown with 100 other boats. It was just too crowded but a
pretty city. We ate Chinese food and Henry got very sick.
March 17 underway Guadalupe
11:00 course 345 sp 6kts wind SE 20
17:00 rounding E side of Domenique
March 18 0900 arrive B Terre, Guadalupe.

Visitors arrive. Ginny Wright, Henry's mother, Charlene Scarf and her
son Matt.

Ginny, Henry, Matt- Guadalupe.

Dock space was at a premium here so we had to tie up to a fishing boat. Our guests were happy to be in paradise but wanted a little better scenery so we agreed on Terre de Houte, a beautiful little island a few hours away. There was nice clean water a few other cruising boats around Everybody swam. A nice sailboat was anchored thirty feet away. They had four kids swimming behind their boat. I spotted a rather large shark swimming on the surface about twenty feet from them with his dorsal fin a foot out of the water. I yelled to the kids. They couldn't hear me. Their mother came on deck. She got their attention. They quickly scrambled into their dingy. That ended the swimming!

We hired a taxi that took us up a mountain that was once a volcano that had erupted many years ago. The crater was a quarter mile wide with lush jungle flora and a beautiful waterfall. Pools of hot baths were all around. We enjoyed the meditative hot water baths and quiet for several hours. A tropical paradise! Then two large buses on a religious retreat appeared. They unloaded what seemed to be hundreds of screaming kids and a few parents. That spoiled the meditative fun so we left.

Charlene and Matt slept on Kudra owned by George, from Atlanta. It was a larger, more comfortable boat. Some fishermen gave us part of their catch which we grilled on Kudra. We celebrated Ginny's 48th birthday while she was there, which was a treat for all of us! We ran out of bottle gas, so the Henrys walked a mile to the nearest fill station. The walk back to TAIS was difficult with the now full can. Henry Jr. gripped the handle with his right hand. I gripped the handle with my left hand and then put my right hand on his right shoulder, suspending the gas can between us. It was a little awkward, but we could carry the heavy bottle gas can in this manner.

ANTIQUA

At 0800 Mar 25 our guests departed by taxi to the airport. It was always sad when friends leave.

At 1300 we sail to Desheyes spend one night. At 0700 Mar 26 we underway Antigua under cruising genoa and reefed main wind NNE at 20.

March 28 1900. We had a race with the sun to reach Carlisle Bay by dark.

We didn't want to enter a strange harbor at night. We raced the last half mile under power and sail smoke streaming. We dropped the anchor just as the sun plopped into the ocean, to the sounds of 30 boats (people) clapping. They all knew.

Sundown at Antigua.

About time for a shave.

Mar 29 0800. Sailed around to English Harbor checked in at customs, spent one night then sailed around to Falmouth Bay one hundred fifty yards off the famous Antiqua Yacht Club. Cruising people like Antigua, especially racers. They have an international race week that is known world-wide. There is a mountain with a flat top where hundreds of people go each night (like Key West) to watch the sun go down over the water then explode before it drops into the sea. Everyone cheers and has another drink.

Our guest, a friend of Jim and Beverly's, arrived just in time to experience this ritual. A nice introduction to the tropics for a city girl.

April 2 1500. Overnight sail to St. Barts.

April 3 1:00. Arrive St Barts

April 4. Underway St. Martin.

April 2nd 1500 hours we cranked in the anchor and heavy chain and set sail bound for St. Barts. We spent one uneventful night on April fourth. We were underway bound for St Marten. 1100 hours we arrived St. Marten. Anchored on the Dutch side. St. Marten is unusual. One half the island is French, the other half Dutch. We had reports that the Dutch side was more friendly. It was very friendly.

We had heard about the nude beach. We all agreed we would try a visit. Our visitor was apprehensive as we were! We locked up TAIS, dingied to the beach and hired a taxi. The beach was pretty ordinary, with usual crystal water, palm trees, a nice breeze and people running around with no clothes on. I had visions of beautiful women, playboy centerfold types, frolicking nude. This was not the case. What we saw was older sagging women and young kids. Seeing ten women sitting on bar stools with their bare butts hanging over is not really sexy. I think they were all watching the naked male bartender in front of them.

Our guest decided she wanted to buy a few trinkets to take home. Two nude men were manning the trinket stand. She was torn with the embarrassment of looking or not looking. She said she got a sheepish peek.

Our passenger was excited because she was a novice. Henry Jr. and I both like teaching so we took turns educating her about do's and don'ts on a boat. Our rules were pretty lax except when it came to our safety or the safety of the boat.

Some of the rules for guests were we are all crewmembers and share lookout all the time when we're not sleeping. Anyone on deck makes a habit of scanning the horizon for ships or land, looking ahead for floating trees, barrels, etc. We had seen fifty five gallon drums partially submerged or half full surfing down a large wave doing twenty miles an hour. Undersail keep your hands and feet away from load bearing lines, winches, chocks, cleats, anything that could hurt.

If you don't know something, ask Henry or me. Nothing is too stupid to ask about. Stay away from electrical stuff and switches and the engine.

By this time, "the Henry's," having been at sea for nine months, were used to where everything was on deck. For example, we could move quickly at night and never step on a cleat. We were like performers in a circus we had practiced so much. I could communicate with Henry Jr. from the cockpit to the foredeck with hand signals. If it was blowing really hard, we couldn't hear a person forty feet away.

We had a pretty heavy following sea and twenty knot winds. Then it rained at night so visibility was lowered and we had to be more vigilant. Our visitor got scared, but she was willing to learn and calmed down when she realized we were calm. I took fixes on the sat nav and plotted them on a chart. She was fascinated at how we always knew where we were. There were some low lying islands about ten miles to starboard, so we didn't want to get blown or set any farther in that direction. In open water there is no reference for tides. If there is a stationary marker, you can see the water rushing by and get a sense of direction and speed.

The rain stopped, and we took turns sleeping. When day break came, I took a fix to see where we were- showed her. She remarked, "How far did we go when we crossed the ocean last night!" We laughed...

BRITISH VIRGIN I. AND VIRGIN ISLANDS

To me the most anxious thing about a nude beach is getting used to your own public nudity. Most are self-conscious at first. Men because their little weenies shrivel up in cold water. Women expose their bosoms which to them are too little or too big. Their butts and thighs are exaggerated. After a while we forgot about that kind of stuff, but it was an interesting experience nevertheless. We also had a wonderful dinner at a French restaurant (not nude).

At 0600 April 4 we set sail for Prickly Pear Cays north of Anguilla. Our cruising buddies said we should stop and snorkel. We did! Prickly Pear had a small entrance and a small anchorage. At 1000 we anchored, pumped up the dingy and put the little motor on the transom. We paddled thirty yards and we were on the reef. There were no other boats, just a beautiful reef five to ten feet deep. The water was clear with thousands of fish and beautiful coral. three hours later we upped anchor, set main, and working jib bound for St. Thomas one hundred miles North West with wind SE 15 kts boat speed 5.5 knots.

April 6 AM: We arrived at St. Thomas and cleared customs. Our guest departed. She did not want to go, she cried and hugged us both. It is so easy to enjoy island life and the sailing life. Most people never experience true relaxation like this.

April 8 TAIS lying at anchor. Charlotte Amalie harbor downtown St. Thomas. My sister Jane and her daughter Jane Blount arrive.

The next day, we sailed to water island. We had good snorkeling in Druid Bay and spent the night. April 10 we sailed back to St. Thomas, then to Saba island then back again. Our snorkeling was often lazy, dingy snorkeling. One would lay on his stomach with mask and snorkel, then lean over the side with head in the water. The other person would idle the little four horsepower Yamaha over the reef.

April 11 we sailed over to Jost Van Dyke in the British Virgins. This is a favorite island for me. We arrive at 1300. Jost Van Dyke is small.

The routine is ridiculous. You dingy to the beach, drag the dingy onto the palm lined beach, then check in customs and immigration.

Henry Jr. took this atop the mast, Jost Van Dyke, B.V.I.

Customs is a small shack about forty feet long divided in half by a solid wall. A large man, we called him Fat Albert- Albert may have been his name, was behind the counter. There were no other employees. Albert was dressed in a military jacket with gold trimming and buttons and a military hat. He looked very official. We paid customs, and Albert stamped our passports. Now Jost Van Dyke only had twenty five residents on the entire island. After customs Albert said we would have to check in with immigration. Where is that? Out the front door five feet down the porch. The other door was immigration. Guess who was behind the counter? You guessed it. Albert. Now, Albert had a different hat, and different jacket with lots of gold. It was his immigration uniform! He walked all of ten feet from customs to immigration. This was a comical experience.

A short walk down the beach is Foxy's. A bar to remember! Jimmy Buffett wrote about Foxy's, which was his favorite too. Foxy's had a fifty foot bamboo thatched hut with a palm frond roof. It was open in the front with a small bar, and half dozen picnic tables. This is Foxy's home and bar. He is a native and a very talented musician. He was shamelessly funny and famous for his relationship with the "Margarita Man." The ceiling at Foxy's is no more than seven foot high. He had a pet monkey that seemed to stay overhead, hidden in the palm fronds. If a patron walks in with yachting cap on, the monkey will hang by his feet in the bamboo thatched ceiling and pull the man's hat off. It is fun for everyone to watch a new yachtsman come into the bar and see the shock on his face when his hat was stolen.

Foxy sat on a picnic table with his guitar, singing island songs. He also composed on the spot. I had been there four or five times and cannot remember what story goes with what visit. I believe Foxy was on the Tonight Show once, jamming with Buffett.

The other bar on Jost Van Dyke is Peace and Plenty. There was no cash register. Patrons keep track of their own drinks and pay when they leave. You shouldn't cruise the Virgins without going to Foxys. I highly recommend it.

Next day we sailed to St. John and anchored in Caneel Bay then Cruz Bay. We sailed to St. Thomas on 13th or 14th, then we sailed the Jane's to Buck I for some fun dingy snorkeling. We enjoyed them and hated to see them leave.

April 16, Suzanne and her dad Nat arrived. We were anchored one hundred fifty yards off downtown St. Thomas. Nat was funny. Henry Jr. brought them out in the dingy. Nat handed me a fifth of Scotch as he came up the ladder. He said, "I am a Hilton man and may not like this." I gave him the aft cabin with double bed and private head. Marine heads are notorious for stopping up. We had our little introduction speech for new visitors. I gave mine to Nat, but he was the kind of guy who didn't follow directions well and the head clogged. It was not much fun cleaning number two out of a marine head.

April 16 we sailed to Megans Bay on the other side of the island where it was nice and quiet. Charlotte Amalie was noisy being downtown, but it was convenient. It got a little choppy sailing around the island and I remember looking over at Nat who was getting splashed with salt spray while hugging the winch for dear life. He was really a good sport though. Next day we sailed back to Charlotte Amalie. Nat treated us to some really nice restaurants. We visited Saba and snorkeled at Buck Island. I believe they had a good time. Henry Jr. had been homesick for Suzanne so they spent some private time together and I got to know Nat a little better. They departed April 21.

April 25 my brother Laurens arrived. That night was a festival. The islanders love their music and celebrations. This was downtown and there were hundreds of people. We were three whites in a sea of black natives. Laurens had not had a drink in years, but that night, being away from Betsy, he "tied one on." It is easy to get separated in a big boisterous crowd. I decided we should meet each hour at a given location. This worked for the first hour. Henry Jr. and I met the second hour. There was no Laurens. We began to get worried. Then shots rang out. The crowd scattered. We were afraid Laurens was involved in some way. In the early AM, most of the people had gone home. Finally we found him sitting with an old native engaged in a very serious conversation. We dragged him away and escorted him to the dingy and on to TAIS.

April 26 we sailed Laurens to Jost Van Dyke- He loved it like everyone else. That night we grilled chicken on our gas grill hanging on the stern rail. Laurens finished a breast. I told him to throw it over board. As soon as it hit the water there was a loud gulp and a thrash. We watched as the next breast was tossed over the port rail. We saw a four foot huge barracuda. The other half was under the boat. Needless to say, he jumped right on the next carcass as soon as it hit the water.

The next morning we dingied to Foxy's. Foxy was in a fun mood. He is partial to sailors. A sixty foot motor yacht came into the harbor and anchored close to us. We watched their expensive dingy hit the water. The owner, an elderly white haired distinguished man, was dressed out in new white pants, white new yachting shoes and a expensive silk shirt and yachting cap. The man was being driven ashore by his captain. Foxy saw all of this and composed a song about the man's clothes. His bill at Abercrombie could feed Foxy for six months. He did not want to get his feet wet. He even threw in his pet barracuda- When the man came to the bar, Foxy stopped singing. The man never knew the song was about him and his money. To top it all off, the monkey stole the man's hat and disappeared into the palm fronds.

Later that day we sailed to Tortola, filled our gas bottles visited with some nice people on a CSY, spent the night and sailed back to St. Thomas. On the way back, Laurens put a feather out and soon a large King Mackeral was on the line. I steered while he and Henry took turns reeling. It was a thirty pound King Mackeral. Henry Jr. and Laurens cut the fish into steaks. We saved a few to grill. They took a cooler full to a seafood market in St. Thomas- the owner would not buy it so they stood outside with the lid open and sold it all to the people passing by. When life is simple this is a nice adventure.

April 30 early AM we departed for Culebra, an interesting friendly island, wrapping around a protecting bay with small mountains, Ensenada Honda. We dingyed in to the little village and asked if there was a restaurant. No English was spoken there. Henry Jr.'s Spanish was good so we were guided to a little white house with screen porch with no restaurant sign. We feasted on nice country food, which always had plantains, but with rice and chicken.

May 1 0900 we up anchor and were underway to Cayo de Louis Pena, a small cove on the west side. We had a great snorkel at noon. Next, we upped anchor en route to Fajardo, on the southern tip of Puerto Rico. We passed a series of large rocks on our starboard side.

PUERTO RICO

P assing about a half mile to starboard, late afternoon we arrived Fajardo and tied up at the customs dock. Peter and Jill on "Zeal" were there already. Laurens dropped over a line at the dock and soon yelled for help. He had hooked some kind of fish that must have weighed two hundred pounds. We were only able to lift his head out of the water before he broke the hook. Laurens was disappointed. He loved catching fish!

At 0900 May 2, we departed Fajardo in the company of "Zeal" bound for San Juan. The water off the Atlantic coast of Puerto Rico is very deep, so we sailed about three miles off the beach. We had a friendly race with "Zeal." Henry changed sails several times then flew the spinnaker. We jumped out about one knot faster and pulled away from "Zeal," just to show her we could. At 1700 hours we entered the breakwater at San Juan to port. There stood an old fort and tourist attraction of old San Juan It had very old high stone walls with parapets and gun mounts built to protect the harbor in old sailing days. To starboard was another wall that housed a leper colony, isolated by the river. We wound around the river with "Zeal" and at 1745 anchored off Club Nautico. We dingyed to Club Nautico after securing TAIS from the days sail. Peter and Jill went with us. We found a nice restaurant, sat down and ordered a cold beer. Good restaurant food was a treat for us because I cooked so much aboard TAIS.

Peter and Jill, our English cruising buddies, "Zeal" in background.

Soon the restaurant got loud mainly because of four guys at a table near us. It was easy to hear what they were talking about. Theirs was a fascinating story. I recognized the accent of one. I asked, "Are you from the N.C Outer Banks?" He said yes. I told him we were from North Carolina too. The four were crew members of a sixty foot long-liner, commercial fishing boat. They had been catching sharks and other fish near Granada. The incident they were describing happened about three am between Calebra and Puerto Rico. A crew member was steering the boat. All the other crew members were asleep. He decided to relieve himself and put the boat on automatic pilot. He opened the door to urinate overboard and suddenly found himself in the water holding on to the door knob that had pulled off! The boat on autopilot continued on course, leaving their crew member in the water. his first thought was "O my God I am dead." He had no life preserver and it was dark. He said he also thought about all of the sharks he had killed and that there might be some strange retribution.

In the moonlight he saw the outline of a tiny rock-island about the size of small house a quarter mile away. His only chance of survival was to swim to this rock. Hours later he made it to the rock terrified of a possible shark attack.

The boat was twenty miles away by now. Could they find him? At first light the captain, awake now, went up to relieve the wheel watch. He saw the open door with no knob and his crew member gone! He quickly turned the boat around put it on a reverse course on auto pilot went down below and woke up the crew to stand look out watch.

A few hours later, the man shivering on the rock saw a tiny speck on the horizon. As the spec grew larger, he said he knew it was his boat. A lookout finally spotted him frantically waving his arms. They retrieved him from the rock. He was saved! These four seamen included us in their celebration. What a great night! Just another example of the common bond that cruising people have.

Laurens stayed a few more days. We really enjoyed having him crew with us. He said it was the best vacation he had ever had. Beverly, my girlfriend, came for a few days. We enjoyed seeing her. Dinners in old San Juan were delicious. We enjoyed black beans and rice at the famous old restaurant, la Zaragozana!.

One evening we were having dinner on deck and saw the carcass of a blue marlin floating nearby. A huge shark came partially out of the water with the carcass in his mouth, then disappeared carcass and all. We just looked at each other and said, "No swimming in these waters." The sport fishing dock was close by. We walked the dock admiring these fine sport fishing boats that would bring in five or ten blue marlin each day. These fish would weigh three hundred to nine hundred pounds. the natives with machetes would filet these giant fish then throw the carcass overboard to float down the river. A great feeding ground for sharks.

TAIS Log: 17:30 up anchor May 13 we topped off water and fueled at Club Nautico

18:30 passed El Morro Abeam to star. Enroute Great Inaqua-Bahamas 800 miles. First way point is 301degrees 166 miles

Crusing under large cruising genoa no main 6 knots wind NE 18 knots

May 14 0120 sterring 300 degrees 6 knots bar 29.76 wind NE 15 kts.

May 15 2000 hours reached waypoint 10 mi Abeam Cape Isabella Santo Domingo wind NE 18 kts sea 8 feet bar 29.75 steady course 295 degrees speed 6knots

1700 course 290 degrees bar 29.7 falling 195 mi to Great Inaqua

May 16 0100 bar steady 29.7 light NE wind started engine 2300 5 kts course 290

1230 wind @ 10 kts NE down cruising genoa up with spinnaker speed 5.6 kts

May 17 0500 sighted Great Inaqua light!

May 18 0800 anchor Great Inaqua- Matthew town.

BAHAMAS

March 17 1300 Checked in customs and immigration. Very very friendly people! Tiny town can walk the entire village in five minutes. We were invited to a small guest house to eat. The best fried chicken since Maurice. Maurice was a wonderful woman who cared for our children and was a wonderful cook.

There was no ice on the island, so the restaurant owner was nice enough to give us some of his private stash. Frozen plastic bowls from his freezer. Great Inaqua was not a tourist spot so was unspoiled and very friendly. We noticed that whenever we went, the less tourists, the more friendly the people were. So many Americans are rude and obnoxious.

TAIS Log:

May 17 1520 underway Long Island southern most island in the Exumas

Waypoint 95 miles 318 degrees under small cruising genoa wind SE 24 kts

2020 change course 345 degrees

May 18 1600 anchor Long Island

May 19 1000 up anchor around s tip of Long island to little San Salvador under small cruising genoa bar 29.8 wind NE 20

May 20 anchor in Horseshoe Bay 0830 wind NE20

We spent all day in and around the water. Little San Salvador, discovered by Columbus, is a treasure. It is small, maybe a three mile wide island, with a very narrow entrance which opens up to a incredible lake. There wasn't a ripple on the water but nice breeze. It had a depth of fifteen feet of the clearest water I have ever seen. We put on mask and fins to check out the bottom of TAIS and found lots of barnacles. Armed with putty knives, we began chipping off the barnacles. The little particles sinking down created an attraction for hundreds of colorful reef fish. They were feeding all over us even nipping at our bathing suits! There were no other boats nor people on this island. We had our own tropical paradise. We spent the day and night here wondering if anyone in the world is this happy. When life is simple, you become more appreciative of nature and natural things like stars. Away from civilization, you feel they are so close you can touch them. Who thinks about the stars at home? We are just too busy and there are too many lights around to spoil the view.

NASSAU

TAIS log: May 21 leave Little San Salvador bound for Eleuthra Governers Harbor going East of Eleuthra c. 020 wind NE 20 under main and small genoa bound for Nassau 1300 hours c. 320 May 22 0600 sight Nassau light off port bow 0900 arrive Nassau

We were just inching our way along enjoying the marine life, like dolphins playing on the bow. Henry Jr. would talk to them. We also saw an occasional whale and sea birds. There are only a few Frigate birds this far north, but lots of pelicans and sea gulls with a clear starry night to guide us with the moon's highway like path.

We stayed a couple days and found Nassau to be very commercial but it also had some good food, good swimming, and lots of partying.

Sunday May 24 at 1500 we pulled up the anchor, made TAIS seaworthy for the open Atlantic and set sail for Wrightsville Beach course. 340 speed 6kts wind a strong 20-25 knots from N.E. bar steady at 29.8 under reefed main and working jib. Waypoint just above Berry Islands NE providence channel.

GOING HOME

TAIS Log: May 24 change course (C.C) 320 waypoint 320 6 mi
BIG SEAS wind 30-35 NE
2215 C.C. 297

0200 sea calmer in the mouth of the ocean. In the dark night, we suddenly saw a blinding light almost on top of us from astern and high above! We were scared to death. Then a loud speaker blasted, "This is the US coast guard. Turn on your radio to channel 16." The captain was thinking about boarding us. We just knew! He wanted to know who we were, where we came from and where we were going. We answered. After a few minutes of nervous conversation, I guess he was satisfied that we were not drug smugglers and allowed us to continue.

Monday 0800 March 25 twenty miles SE of Freeport with the wind moderated some, we had sailed all night, wet with spray. Under reefed main and the workhouse working jib bar steady 29.8.

May 26 1400 wind NE 20 working jib and reefed main course 000 due north punching into BIG SEAS but with the help of the Gulf Stream we are making 7knots.

May 26 1900 sixty five miles off Daytona Beach. We spotted a U.S. navy helicopter coming low towards us.

He circled us several times for a few minutes and then we got a radio call, "TAIS, TAIS, This is the U.S.S. Forrestal. The captain speaking."

"U.S.S. Forrestal this is TAIS, good afternoon, captain."

"TAIS, where have you been and where are you going?"

"We crossed the Atlantic in December, been sailing the islands working our way north to Wrightsville Beach North Carolina, our home."

"Good Henry. Sounds like a great trip. Stay on your present course you will be fine. I'll have my flock in in a few minutes and we will return to base. Enjoyed talking with you. Have safe passage."

"Thank you captain."

We could see the huge carrier now and the little planes one by one landing on her deck. Talking to that captain was like talking to a next door neighbor, very casual, not what you expect from the captain of the Forrestal!

We talked on the radio to a sailboat twenty five miles east of us. He overheard the previous conversation. He said the seas were very big and how was it where we were? I think we were a little better off, so he decided to sail a little west too. The Gulf Stream at five plus knots runs north. When the wind blows hard from the NE against the Gulf Stream it creates very big steep waves with rolling breakers, a dangerous situation.

That night the wind was thirty knots from NE creating scary steep seas. We decided to take down the working jib and put up the storm jib. Henry remembers this night too. I had forgotten about the deck lights. A flood light was mounted on each spreader pointing down to shine on the deck. These lights were of great value underway at night for changing headsails. This night was very black, no moon, no stars, the Captain turns the deck lights on so Henry can go forward and reduce sail. A benefit of twin forestays, in this case, the working jib was flying but the wind got too strong for it. The storm jib was attached to the other forestay and lashed to the deck. Henry had to drop the working jib, secure it, and raise the storm jib. The captain had to steer Tais into the wind to accomplish this. I started the engine, put it in gear to keep headway. The lights flooding the deck contrasted with total blackness above and below except for spray and white huge breaking waves. This creates a different and eerie scene for those on board. I've said before your mind plays tricks on you at night, your senses change, sounds you didn't hear during the day, you hear at night. It's part of our survival instinct, you give up one sense and another tries to compensate. Henry remembers having to crab crawl, hooked to harness and lifeline, to the fore deck to change these sails. He says he was holding on for "dear life" to the bow sprit, with one hand and wrestling with sails with the other. All the while riding up the face of twenty foot steep waves, then dropping off the backside of the wave. This would make his stomach drop each time, like riding a rollercoaster. Even though he was wearing a harness, going overboard in heavy seas would not be a good thing, because you would likely be beaten up against the side of the boat until you were hauled in. I remember watching him carefully as he crawled back into the safe cockpit. Then exhausted, he said "There is not a ride at Carowinds that can compare to that!" With the storm jib up we fell off to leeward, the sails filled up and Tais became much more comfortable and stable, sailing with the wind off our starboard bow rather than head on. I was very proud of how he handled himself on that maneuver. We talked a lot about what a humbling feeling we had being far from land for days, knowing that Mother Nature could splinter Tais into little pieces if she wanted to. The more time we spent at sea, the more respect we gained for its' immense power. I think that's why it is such a kick to be able to control this power for your own use.

The seas subsided considerably when we went further west on May 28 0500 we were forty five miles east of Charleston. Seas were now eight foot instead of fifteen, wind was down to twenty back now to reefed main and working jib.

About two am we changed course for a more direct route to the mouth of the Cape Fear River. Home at last! We could see the Oak Island light about fifteen miles out. We were motor sailing with working jib to aim for the light. The lighthouse is actually a little south and west of Bald Head at the entrance.

I have fished these waters since I was a boy. I love these waters. Wonderful frying pan shoals, breaking water from Bald Head all the way east about twenty eight miles to the end, signified by a manned light tower to warn sailors of the dangerous shoals. We drew too much water to cross the shoals. Too many boats and ships lay wrecked on these treacherous shoals. Fishing, trolling in and out of the sleughs in daylight is fun in a small seaworthy boat. It is not fun at night in a sailboat whose keel is six feet deep.

We decided to go into the Cape Fear river. The entrance, guarded by Bald Head to starboard and Civil War Fort Caswell to port, was deep and wide. We thought it would be an easy entrance since big ships came in and out. It was about four am. Should we wait for daylight? Or go ahead. We were both exhausted after three plus days at sea being beat up by huge waves and high winds. We decided to go in, just motor on in. I know this river, so I thought and decided to break one of my cardinal rules: "Don't enter a new port at night." We found the sea buoy, passed it.

The things about night visual navigation is that you lose your depth perception. You cannot always see the green light buoys or their distance from the red ones. The red ones mark the right side of the channel "red right returning" the green or black. The left side. The best course is to stay in the middle.

We didn't! Ran aground! I slammed against the wheel, Henry slammed against the house. TAIS, for the first time in days, was dead in the water as the saying goes.

We had several questions: Was the tide rising or falling? Could we get off? Was the bottom sand or mud? With a spot light we could see the inlet ocean current moving towards the river. Good! That meant the tide was rising!

Together we made a plan of action to get off of this sandbar. When a sailboat runs aground the keel plows a trench. It is difficult, if not impossible, to turn the boat around with the six foot keel imbedded in this trench it has dug for itself. We tried backing out, the way we came in. Nothing doing. Our little fifty horsepower diesel was not strong enough for the job. Sometimes, you can put a sail up and sail off but that night there was no wind.

We pumped up the dingy and I suggested Henry try something different. We dropped the pumped up dingy overboard with the little outboard attached and a line: Henry Jr. got in. I pulled him around to the bow. I unhooked the TAIS forty five CRQ anchor and lowered it into the dingy. He moved toward the stern on a reverse track with the anchor and one hundred fifty foot of heavy chain. The weight of the anchor plus its chain almost sank the small dingy. He finally dropped the anchor overboard almost behind TAIS, tied up the dingy astern, and came back aboard TAIS. Then we put the chain around the winch (windlass) and slowly cranked the bow around facing the way we came in. I put the engine in gear, full throttle as he winched. Slowly TAIS began to move. I throttled back. We were floating! We did not pull the anchor up because we didn't know where we were.

We had passed a freighter waiting offshore before our mishap. I told Henry she was probably waiting for a pilot. A pilot is a local person who is trained in ship maneuvers with local knowledge of the river. He takes temporary command of the ship to bring her upriver and dock her. The captain is usually by his side. The forty foot pilot boat came fifty yards from us en route to the freighter. I called him on the ship radio. He answered and said he saw us. I told him our plight. He said, "When I pick up this ship and come in the inlet, pull in behind me." Half an hour later, here she came, the ship doing about fifteen knots. We could only do six. We pulled in behind and followed as best we could till we were in the river. We were relieved to see dawn break. We tied up at the tiny town of Southport. We went to a restaurant full of fishermen. We had not seen soap and water for three days so we smelled pretty bad. We didn't know who might be waiting for us at Wrightsville. We each took a bird bath in the bathroom, ate a huge breakfast, our only hot food for days. I was embarrassed at having run aground after a 12,000 mile voyage in my own backyard.

The next thirty miles was working jib and motoring up the river then the intracoastal waterway north to my cousin Jim's beach house on Wrightsville Beach. We dropped a stern anchor and tied the bow to his pier. A customs agent was waiting. He would not let us off until he inspected the boat and our papers. He was interested in our trip after he cleared us. He confiscated some fruit we bought in the Bahamas. We were not allowed to bring any fruit into the U.S.

TAIS at Wrightsville Marina after 12,000 miles.

We were met by a writer, John Vaughn, and a photographer, Don Sturkey, from The Charlotte Observer. He wanted to feature The Henry's for Father's Day Sunday paper. A full three page spread!

We were very tired, but the photographer, Don Sturkey, wanted to take pictures at sea. He got in my cousins boat with a driver. We untied TAIS pulled up the stern anchor and put up the main and cruising genoa and headed out to sea. After pictures, we sailed back in. I could remember, a year before, this was a big production. Now we could set sail almost in our sleep. It's amazing what repetition and memory does for confidence.

I had a two hour lunch with John Vaughn. I told him about our trip. He wrote a really nice article about father and son. Our family gave us a big party, close to fifty friends and family, at the Bishop's house. The Observer guys stayed for that. What a nice ending from our year at sea!

HOME

A certain sadness overcame me, realizing our year long voyage covering 12,000 miles was almost over. A part of me did not want it to end. I would have to go back to work! Who wants that?!

A boat can be a sacred space, because life is lived and experiences shared in such a small space of the cabin or the open space of the sea and sky as it comes to meet the sea. Henry Jr. and I will never share the solitude of love, compassion, energy, and dependency on each other again. I am sometime jealous of that time. But selfishness gives way to love and to his independence. He is all grown up and I am so proud of him. To watch someone grow and know that you had a little something to do with it is one of life's great winners.

Courtesy of The Charlotte Observer

Courtesy of The Charlotte Observer

Charlotte Observer Article

Vaughn, John. "Captain Dad." *The Charlotte Observer.* 21 June 1987.7-8E. Print. Photos by Don Sturkey.

Captain Dad

"Henry Wright sold his car, raided his savings account, left behind a sales job and took to the sea with his 19-year-old son. During their year-long odyssey, they came to understand and to respect each other as never before."

On this Father's day, Henry Wright and his 19-year-old son, Henry Jr., are struggling to re-enter a world of schedules and structured time that they abandoned, together, one year ago.

Their readjustment isn't proving easy.

For 12 months father and son shared the cramped, tossing cabin of a 41-foot sailing sloop in the Mediterranean, Atlantic and Caribbean – eating only when they were hungry, sleeping only when they could, oblivious to the passage of days.

On the 12,000-mile voyage they lived amid sudden squalls and sunlit seas, coasting among green tropical islands, dropping anchor in white harbor towns beside turquoise waters.

The sense of unreality was still with them two days later, as they talked about their cruise from the porch of a Wrightsville cottage.

"I'm feeling disoriented," says Henry Sr., 52. "I know I'm here, but I'm not entirely here." It was "sort of like a dream," says his son. "We've been on the move so long I feel like we should be getting ready to move on now."

It's not just the sea life they're missing now. During the cruise father and son developed a deep respect for one another, an intimate understandin of each other's strrenghts and weaknesses. Now they miss that man-to-man intimacy.

I'm sure Henry saw some sides of me he hadn't seen much befre – weak sides," the father says. "We all have dark sides, and there's no keeping that from a child in such close circumstances."

The cruise was a lifelong dream of Henry Sr., who used to walk the docks of Wrightsville Beach as a boy, watching itinerant sailboats coming in for the night.

Eighteen months ago he felt the time was ripe for what he calls "the ultimate getaway." He had recently divorced after 20 years of marriage, and was temporarily burned out in his sales career. His daughter Virginia, 21, was deeply involved in college life and didn't want to make the trip. His son Henry was about to graduate from high school and dreamed, like his father, of going to sea in a small boat.

Their decision was made in the winter of 1986, after the two talked with several round-the-world sailors at a meeting of their Slocum

Society in Annapolis, Md. Last June, after four months of planning, the two Charlotteans flew to Spain, bought their nine-year-old sailboat and rechristened is Tais. The name means world traveler in Polynesian.

During the voyage Henry Sr. saw his son grow from a boy into a man.

"It was a joy to see him do thing he could do better than I," he says. "Henry is better at celestial navigation than I am, for instance; I learned never to question his math. It's nice to be able to rely on someone totally."

★★★

Tais log, July 13, 1986, off Gibraltar: *Hen misses working out with his weights, so he does chin-ups and pull-ups...I'm very proud of the way he's accepting his responsibilities. Our lives depend on each other. As the saying goes: "This ain't no dress rehearsal; this is it."*

★★★

Henry Jr. said he saw a softer side of his father on the long voyage – and a tougher side he's rarely seen before.

"In stressful situation he stayed calm and kept a clear head. I never saw him panic when things were rough. I have a lot of respect for the risks he took."

And what were those risks? Financial, to begin with.

Henry Wright had worked as a sales agent for eight companies between Charlotte and New York. When he told his employers he'd decided to take a year off to realize a lifelong dream, seven of the eight told him he would lose his sales territories. He left anyway.

He and his former wife, Virginia, sold a house they owned jointly, and he invested his half of the equity in the sailboat. That was about $50,000. He also found someone to rent his condo. He sold his BMW and all the stock he owned, and withdrew his savings. When he returned from his year at sea last month he had to start from scratch, with no certainty of a job.

Wright figures he's put $75,000 into the boat, counting repairs. The voyage itself cost another $15,000. The trip's expenses, he says, were worth the sacrifice.

"We've both met a lot of who said: 'I wish my father rand I could have done something like that,'" he says. "Most women I know didn't particularly like the idea of the cruise. But most of the men said: 'Do it.'"

That's not what his accountant said.

Wright's accountant said he was crazy. "But that's rational thinking, "says Wright, "and rational people don't do thing like this. I make a lot of decisions on gut feeling."

Virginia Wright, Henry Jr.'s mother, wasn't exactly thrilled at the prospect of her going to the sea in a boat the size of a large living room.

"I was terrified they'd be lost at sea," she says. "But mixed with the fear was excitement. It was a wonderful opportunity for Henry (Jr.). How many people get to do something like that? I was terrified but I was excited."

Their Mediterranean course took the wrights from Gandia, Spain to Majorca, then to Sardinia, up the northern coast of Sicily to Messina, into the Adriatic and spent five days in Rome before flying home to attend a coming-out party for daughter Virginia.

Resuming the voyage six days later, the Henrys passed several days on Madeira, off northern Africa. Henry Sr. calls the Portuguese island "probably the most impressive place on the entire trip." The Mediterranean cruise ended in the Canary Islands.

* * *

Tais log, July 30, 1986: *We're pretty much over our queasiness now and can eat most anything we want. Our fresh veggies are gone now; so is the ice. This life is so much like camping: salt-water baths from a bucket, then rinse with a little fresh water. We entered Milazzo (Siciliy) at eight in the evening just before dark...*

* * *

The Wrights crossed the Atlantic in 19 days, one of 210 yachts in a transatlantic race sponsored by rum distillery in Barbados. (Tais was number 52 across the finish line.)

Besides much canvas, the sloop carried a 60-horseppower diesel engine, an Aries wind vane for self-steering, satellite navigation equipment, a ham radio and four-person life raft.

The boat has a topside center cockpit, two toilets, a sofa, dinette, navigation table, cooking range, beds fore and aft. The Wrights took along an electric generator, a small TV and VCR.

But they never watched TV. The read books instead. Carlos Castaneda, John D. MacDonald and Richard Bach ("Bridge Across Forever") were favorite authors. After dinner, amid the vastness of the sea and the star-studded night, they talked about the meaning of life.

* * *

Tais log, Aug. 3: *We're halfway across the Ionian Sea now, about 125 miles out from the Sothern tip of Italy. Except for a few playful dolphins around the bow, we haven't seen*

another living thing: no ships or boats in two
days.

We get into philosophy, it seems after supper
each night…Usually the father doesn't depend on
a son for much. This year it's almost 50-50,
with the ultimate responsibility being mine.

★★★

The Henrys arrived in Barbados Dec. 17 to
begin the Caribbean half of their cruise.
It took them from Barbados to Tobago, then
Venezuela, through the Grenadines, Lesser
Antilles and Virgin Islands, up to Puerto
Rico, the Bahamas, to Eleuthera and Little San
Salvador.

During the long voyage, broken by porty stays
of a week or more, father and son shared the
watches: one slept three of four hours while
the other sat topside in the cockpit under the
sails, listening to whisper of waves astern,
watching for large ships that could run them
down.

An egg timer reminded them to check the
horizon every 15 minutes, day and night, for
large vessels. During heavy weather they
occasionally went two days without sleep,
listening in the darkness to the roar of 40-
knot winds and the sea-serpent hiss of 20-foot
waves.

"I'd read these stories about rogue waves that tare three or four times bigger than the others," says Henry Sr. "They come from a different direction. You hear their hissing and you're compelled to turn around and look, though there's nothing you can do about them."

Such waves can easily damage or capsize a small boat.

The Wrights wore medicinal patches behind their ears to ward off seasickness, but occasionally got seasick anyway.

During the cruise they observed two unalterable rules: No one left the cockpit for any purpose without first waking the other person; and no one moved about the boat without tethering himself to a lifeline.

"If you go overboard in the Atlantic at night in 20-knot winds, you're gone," says Henry Sr.

The TV and VCR proved invaluable – though not as a source of entertainment.

In the Mediterranean, early in the voyage, they couldn't get the math right on their celestial reckonings. One second's error in calculating latitude would put them a mile off course, so accuracy was vital. They finally corrected their error by watching a videotape on celestial navigation, made by writer William Buckley, an avid sailor.

Parents, says Henry Sr., "have a way of looking over their children's shoulders. Hen and I got a point where I didn't do that at all. We communicated almost without words, working together. I saw him grow up into a reasoning person, a problem-solving person."

One of the earliest problems Henry Jr. solved occurred last October, 200 miles off the coast of Africa. Sighting dark storm clouds, the sailors started to reduce sail. But the sails got tangled and couldn't be lowered. Rising winds threatened to blow out the sail.

Henry Jr. climbed into the rope-supported bos'n's chair, scaled the 54-foot mast and disentangled the forestays, while the wind pitched the boat wildly from side to side. Henry Sr. says he could never have done the job. "I'm scared to death of heights."

But he was always in command. "We were and are buddies," he says, "but just as there has to be a captain on a boat, I have to maintain a father relationship with Hen. He knows how far he can go with me."

★★★

Tais log, 100 miles southwest of Grenada, Feb. 8, 1987: *There are hundreds of frigate birds here, mostly black, with swept-back wings three to four feet long…When a frigate bird gets tired of fishing he will find an upward*

air draft and circle and circle until he's
completely out of sight or in the clouds. Our
life is so simple now; we can watch these birds
for hours and not be bored.

* * *

Throughout the voyage they caught marlin, king mackerel, tuna, wahoo, bonita and dolphin (the first, not the aquatic mammal) from lines dragged astern. Whales surfaced around them, one 60-footer coming within 30 yards of Tais.

Twice they became entrapped in fishermen's nets and lost hours trying to find their way out. Twice they were nearly run down by large ships. Once they went far off course at night in heavy weather, and twice they found themselves nearly on the rocks before altering course.

But they had no accidents and no injuries – only scratches and bruises from bumping into bulkheads, doors and tables aboard Tais.

Their worse mishap was the theft in Spain of several thousand dollars, their wallets, passports, a Nikon camera and six rolls of exposed film. Henry Sr. couldn't replace the camera, and the lost money meant few meals could be eaten in restaurants during the remainder of the trip. Fortunately, the older man is an accomplished cook, and there was no shortage of fresh fish.

The night before making landfall at Wrightsville they celebrated Henry Jr.'s 19th birthday with a last hot meal aboard: fried mackerel caught by Hen, cole slaw, beer and a pot of grits.

Home now, father and son are treasuring the weeks before they must part. Henry Sr. is looking for while his prepares for college at UNC-Chapel Hill. The Henrys, as they came to known among the cruising fraternity, may never again be so close.

"What we're both realizing is that we've been so close that we're going to miss each other very much," says Henry Sr. "Hen will be away at school and I'll be hustling to get a little money. There'll never be a tremendous closeness between us, but we'll miss each other."

Wright might sell Tais, or live aboard her a while, or charter her in the Caribbean. He hasn't decided. Hen doesn't want the boat sold, however. "It would be like losing a part of myself," he says. "It was home for a whole year."

And it was the birthplace of memories that will last a lifetime.

***

Tais log: *The days are hazy and the nights black except for the stars. With nothing but the sky and water, it makes us feel very small in this great world. We're just a speck. Henry (Jr.) wonders why we worry about what other people think. We are very close...*

To my Dad,

*There is really no way to fully express on paper the gratitude I feel
for you making the Henry's journey happen. When we first talked
about going on the trip, I was a 17 year old kid, just finishing high
school with a chance to be on a boat and not have to go to school for
a whole year. Sounded like a pretty good deal to me! I don't think
either one of us really knew what we were getting into. Now that
I am 44 years old and have a career and family, I appreciate even
more the risk that you took to make the trip happen. There are lots
of people out there who say things like, "I wish I could do something
like that" or "I wish I had the time or money to take a year off".
The reality is that there are not many people out there who have the
courage to take that "leap of faith" and actually make what was
a lifelong dream of yours actually happen. We saw some amazing
places and experienced some incredible adventures but the love and
friendship and bond that we shared that year at sea was the best part
of the journey and is what I am and will always be most grateful for.*

Henry Jr.

Made in the USA
Columbia, SC
16 November 2022

71431300R00113